FROM CO DOWN

Edited by Emma Marsden

First published in Great Britain in 2000 by
YOUNG WRITERS
Remus House,
Coltsfoot Drive,
Woodston,
Peterborough, PE2 9JX
Telephone (01733) 890066

HB ISBN 0 75431 846X
SB ISBN 0 75431 847 8

FOREWORD

This year, the Young Writers' Future Voices competition proudly presents a showcase of the best poetic talent from over 42,000 up-and-coming writers nationwide.

Successful in continuing our aim of promoting writing and creativity in children, our regional anthologies give a vivid insight into the thoughts, emotions and experiences of today's younger generation, displaying their inventive writing in its originality.

The thought, effort, imagination and hard work put into each poem impressed us all and again the task of editing proved challenging due to the quality of entries received, but was nevertheless enjoyable. We hope you are as pleased as we are with the final selection and that you continue to enjoy *Future Voices From Co Down* for many years to come.

CONTENTS

Clare McCann	53
Ashleigh Kennedy	54
Lyndsey Pentland	55
Sarah Turley	56
Lynsey Beatty	57
Samantha Murphy	58

Beechlawn School

Henry James Abernethy	59
David Curry	59
Fiona O'Neill	59
Seaneen McLaughlin	60
Jonathan Bell	60
Jennifer Graham	61
Andrew Irwin	61

Campbell College

Conor Holmes	62

Down Academy

Steven Beers	62
Suzanne Hobday	63
Andrew Houston	63
Roseanne Johnston	64
Mark Andrews	64
Amy Murray	65
Sara Price	66
Sarah Carlile	66
Lynda McSpadden	67
Holly Douthwaite	68
Anna Smith	68
Sarah Smith	69
Tanya Hamilton	69
Daniel Mills	70
Ross Breen	70
Jane Thomas	71
Ryan Douglas	71
Michael Thomson	72

James Gordon   72

Glenlola Collegiate School
Alanna Kerr	73
Emma Morris	74
Gemma Loughlin	74
Janine Brown	75
Stephanie McFarland	75
Dale Maginnes	76
Keri Connolly	77
Claire Long	78
Laura McIlmurray	78
Catherine Bell	79
Claire MacDonald	80
Laura Murray	80
Jenny McIlhatton	81
Megan Gray	82
Karen McKee	84
Linda Coulter	86
Catriona Holmes	87
J Monson	88
Jane McDowell	89
Elizabeth Patterson	90
Emma Hanna	91
Beth Rodgers	92
Jane Noble	93
Sarah McVeigh	94
Sonya Moorhead	94
Victoria Nelson	95
Kathryn McNair	95
Joanne Elliott	96
Esther Kyle	96
Rachel Gibson	97
Laura Kirkpatrick	98
Lynne Chalmers	98
Helen Baker	99
Tracy Knox	100
Allie McAuley	100

Regent House School

St Colman's High School, Ballynahinch

Gareth McGreevy	177
Conor Trainor	178
John Rooney	179
Damian Ritchie	180
Edwin McKibben	180
Adam Wilson	181
Brendan Scullion	181
Colman Trainor	182
Christopher Sharvin	182
William Russell	183
Christopher Tumelty	184
Shane McAnearney	185
David Gregge	185

Sacred Heart Grammar School

Eleanor Cassidy	185
Denise McGuigan	186
Dervla Lynchehaun	187
Siobhan McNulty	188
Bronagh McNally	189
Jane Rooney	190
Danielle Holsgrove	191
Ciara Connolly	192
Geraldine Trainor	192
Ann-Louise McCamley	193
Andrea Murtagh	194
Judy Black	194
Judith McLogan	195
Aoife McCoy	196
Mairead McCarry	196
Una Montgomery	197
Sara-Louise Cooper	198
Carrie-Anne O'Riordan	198
Billie Phipps-Tyndall	199
Emma Kelly	200
Donna Mc Cartan	200
Joanne Mulholland	201
Aisling Gallagher	202

The Poems

ANDREW

A ndrew is my name
N ever call me Andy
D rew is the nickname I like
R acing motorbikes is the best sport
E specially when it is dirty and
W et.

Andrew Fealty (14)
Ardmore House School

CHRIS

C hris is my name and I don't like work
H arry is my dad's name and he likes golf
R ebecca is the youngest in my family
I like golf and fishing and a lot of other
S ports.

Chris Jordan (13)
Ardmore House School

JOY

Joy is bright green
Joy tastes like a juicy plum
Joy smells like sweet flowers
Joy looks like a green meadow
Joy sounds like waves splashing against the rocks
Joy feels like a cuddly teddy.

Christina Kathleen Walton (12)
Bangor High School

THE FOUR SEASONS

Spring is like a breath of fresh air
and newborn lambs leap into the air.
Flowers are dancers in the breeze
and leaves are growing on the trees.

Summer is like strawberries and cream,
because it is such fun it is a good dream.
The sun is a light bulb in the sky,
too bright to look at with the human eye.

Autumn is like a world of gloom,
as it knows winter is to follow soon.
The trees' leaves turn golden brown
and are feathers which fall to the ground.

Winter is like a dark dreary cellar
and fierce winds blow through all the weather.
Frost, sleet, snow and rain
are soldiers that march to that season again.

Ashleigh McCullough (12)
Bangor High School

MILLENNIUM

The clock of time is ticking, it's almost here,
The year two thousand, the millennium year.
As it draws near, the momentum grows,
What will happen? Nobody knows.

Celebrations that are planned, help hide the fear,
That prophets foretold, Earth's destruction is near.
The Millennium Bug, the world on hold
Earthquakes, volcanoes, the Bible foretold.

The ozone layer growing, wars ravish the land,
The Earth is being destroyed by man's own hand.
Meteorites hurtle towards us from space,
Are these the things the world must face.

I sit and wonder if it will all come to be,
I guess we'll just have to wait and see.
The clock of time is ticking, it's almost here,
The year two thousand, the millennium year.

Leah Stenning (13)
Bangor High School

LEAVING HOME

I don't want to go!
Worried,
Sad,
lonely,
I don't want to go!

I don't want to go!
New teachers,
New school,
New friends,
I don't want to go!

I don't want to go!
Old house,
Old neighbours,
Old friends,
I don't want to go!

Emma Lougheed (11)
Bangor High School

MY FIRST LESSON

Waking up early in the morning
Half asleep while eating my breakfast
Trailing myself into school
Getting my books out for the first lesson
Watching the teacher talk away
While my eyes nearly shut
She asks me a question . . .
Suddenly I am wide awake
What should I do?
I sit there silently waiting for help
The teacher is getting cross now
She asks me again
Now everybody is staring at me
Trying to give me a clue
The clock is ticking
The pressure is on
Finally some help!
Someone else answers
The trouble is over
There is a God!

Sarah Jaffrey (13)
Bangor High School

LOVE!

Love is when you just can't sleep,
Then you know you're in so deep,
Love is when you're walking on air
You think of him while in a stare.

Love is the tingling you feel inside
And you know you are his future bride,
He'll always be the one for you,
The one who will always be true.

Love is like a dream,
In a world of strawberries and cream,
Love is when you have no cares,
Love is soft, cuddly teddy bears.

Love is caring, sharing and giving,
Love is what makes life worth living,
Love is a magical sensation,
A masterpiece of God's creation!

Leigh Ruddock (13)
Bangor High School

MOVING

Devastated!
How dare they?
Why?
When?
Devastated!

Shocked and scared!
Hello new house
New school, new friends.
Goodbye old house and old friends
Shocked and scared!

Nervous!
To meet new teachers,
To meet new people,
To meet new neighbours,
Nervous!

Aleste Lai (11)
Bangor High School

DEVOTED!

Rachel
Last night in the park,
Your eyes were shining and glimmering in the dark.
You looked so handsome and sweet
While my party were advancing at just a few feet.

Richard
Last night in the park,
You looked so lovely in the dark,
With my tattered picture in my wallet of you,
Thinking of my love in whatever I do.
Behind us in the bushes,
My friends started a game of pushes,
I wanted to say goodbye,
But my gang and coolness tore me away,
While my heart and instinct told me to say
I love you!

Nicola Lucas (11)
Bangor High School

HOME SWEET HOME

I'm all alone,
In this desolate house,
The gate hinge squeaking
As I search for the mouse.

The dishes are stacked
I'm not in the mood,
I'm glad in a sense
I can roam in the nude.

There's a knock at the door
And a ring of the bell,
As I cautiously look
To find it's old aunt Sel.

I invite her in
So I'm not alone,
She'll keep me company
In my big, empty home!

Sarah Plummer (13)
Bangor High School

HOW DARE THEY?

We are moving
But why?
Where?
My friends
How dare they?

The school?
The uniform?
Rules?
The teachers?
The school?

The house?
The people?
The neighbours
The place
We are moving.

Jacqueline Lawther (12)
Bangor High School

WE ARE MOVING

We are moving,
angry,
scared,
upset,
shocked,
worried,
we are moving.

We are moving,
away from my friends,
my house,
my room,
how dare they make me move?

We are moving,
new school,
new house,
new room,
we are moving.

Rachel McFarland (11)
Bangor High School

I HAVE A DREAM!

I have a dream in love galore,
Blessed with delight that's never been felt before,
In happiness, friendship and a lot, lot more,
But who can tell what's behind each door.

And so no one knows what the future will hold,
Whether another world war is to behold,
Or whether elephants' tusks will continue to be sold,
After all it's just a minority who have a heart of gold.

Joy is brief as summer is fun,
Happiness this race has not yet run,
One day gods and kings will come,
And the suffering of man will be finished by a gun.

Though in my dream all is not lost,
Our world can still be warm without frost,
In my dream happiness does not cost,
For every bridge has already been crossed.

Ashley Kerr (14)
Bangor High School

SPACE

Planets, different colours
like marbles in a jar
The glittering sun so yellow
looks so near yet far
Shooting stars and comets
whizzing through the night
The moon a giant button
what a beautiful sight.

Never-ending stars
as bright as fairy lights
And numerous minute planets
from near and far away
I wish I really could be there
up in the wonders of space
For if I could be that special one
to go to a special place.

Melissa Amanda-Jane Stenning (12)
Bangor High School

COLD

In the park we sat all day
and watched the world go by
'Fresh air will do you good my dear'
pipes up the woman in white.

How would she know?
She doesn't even realise
that even with two woolly winter sweaters,
a cosy crotchet blanket and small sheepskin slippers
we still feel like blocks of ice.

'So what?' that's what you're thinking, right?
It's alright for you
your body is as fit as a fiddle
your body doesn't feel Jack Frost's
freezing fingers sending that cold sensation
from your head to your toes.

They bring out the flasks of warm sweet tea
just what I need to warm me up.
'Like some tea love?' her tiny voice squeaks.

Never mind your stupid tea
I'll tell you what I'd really like
I'd like heaven's doors to open,
to open really wide and to swallow me up.
Forever, to never let me out
that way I'll never be cold again!

Alex Tipping (14)
Bangor High School

HIM AND ME

He stood there,
I stood here,
As he came near,
I got frustrated with fear.

I didn't know what to say,
I didn't know what to do,
I gazed into his eyes of blue,
But still didn't have a clue.

As he moved closer,
He took my hand,
So we walked hand in hand,
Along the gorgeous yellow sand.

He stopped and stared
And so I glared.
It was almost as if destiny had made us a pair,
Which seemed as fair, as fair can be.

He put his arms around me,
I did so too,
It was almost like a dream come true.

As he pressed his lips against mine,
There was a weird sensation, like a 'bang',
Then after that I was feeling kind of fine.

Laura McKimm (14)
Bangor High School

WHO CARES?

I feel so trapped and hidden away,
Like the sun on a cold winter's day.
The light's been switched off within my heart,
My whole world just seems to have fallen apart.
It's so difficult to find the words to express,
How my hopes have gone and left emptiness.
My dreams are shattered and my thoughts keep spinning round,
So I keep my head low, my eyes fixed on the ground.

Things have all just gone too far,
They'll leave me with a lifelong scar.
I do try and lead a good, moral life,
But I constantly end up in a lot more strife.
There was no indication things weren't going well,
It's like I carry a bad luck spell.
'Cause all of a sudden, just out of the blue,
My mum walked out taking my life with her too.

After 16 years, she's out in the world again,
Shooting tiny arrows which cause great pain.
She doesn't care about anyone else,
She thinks solely of her heartless self.

So here I am, I'm all uptight,
'cause day after day, it's fight after fight.
I'm in my old cave and I've locked the door,
I don't want people to watch as I lie on the floor.
Just dreaming of how my life used to be,
Things I took for granted like the family watching TV.
But all they can be are dreams and no more,
'Cause things have changed so the tears start to pour.

But, like my dreams, this poem must come to an end,
Unlike my life which continues round this awkward bend.
But when I grow old and perhaps have children,
I won't look to my past, I'll be a mum in a million.

Julie Anne McConnell (15)
Bangor High School

THE DISEASE OF AGE

Old age,
The disease that is spreading rapidly,
No cure.
Every day counts, as this disease cunningly creeps up on you.
The disease that nobody wants,
The disease that everybody gets.
The symptoms of greying hair and wrinkles,
The once so young and lively body,
Is now so old and frail.
The face that once gleamed with happiness and love,
Is now crumpled and lonely.
You have to be a special person
To dig through the wrinkles and grey hair.
To search what's inside than sniggering at the outside.
One day the sniggering will stop.
When the people who sniggered will regret it,
As they will be the one being sniggered at,
When they discover the lotions and potions don't work,
When their body starts to decay,
The disease has reached them,
They are growing old.

Lauren Compton (14)
Bangor High School

CAMP

As we climb up the trees,
Going through all the leaves,
Falling onto our tent,
We are glad that we came here.

Climbing the rocks,
Having some rusty knocks,
Bits of rocks falling down,
We are glad that we came here.

Swinging on the rocks,
Getting some rusty burns,
Falling into dirty mud,
We are glad we came here.

Enjoying camp is the best,
Better than all the rest.
Coming home is not fun,
But I would go there again.

Andrew Pritchard (12)
Bangor High School

BOYZONE

B rilliant
O utrageous
Y oung and good
Z ippy
O ut of this world
N ice
E xcellent

Amanda Peters (12)
Bangor High School

THE MONSTER IN MY ROOM

Darkness fell upon me,
I crept up to my room,
Knowing I was in for a long night.
As the rain slithered silently down the window,
The wind hissed and the thunder banged,
I went into my room and checked about,
But all I could find was nought.

I crept slowly into my bed and lay thinking for a while,
What it would be like if there really was
One of those horrible, slimy, drippy creatures
Which are called monsters,
Really under my bed.

I woke up during the night,
And saw monster shadows on my wall.
I let out a squeaky scream *aaaahh!*
That deafened them all.
Suddenly the light clicked on,
My mum came in and said,
'You have had a dreadful dream, try to get back to bed.'

Stephen Lewis (13)
Bangor High School

MY HOLIDAY

Sand as soft as silk
Swimming pool is freezing cold
Sweltering summer sun
Fish are flapping and flopping in the sea
What a wonderful holiday for me!

Natalie Moffett (13)
Bangor High School

SCHOOL

School is like a prison
full of bars and cells
it is as dark as night
with a bit of light.
School is an education centre.
School's scary
with shouting teachers
people's feet go thumpety-thump
school makes the clouds creep in,
quietly.

Alison McKnight (12)
Bangor High School

BLACK!

The colour black is dull
People associate it with death
Black is colourless
Black is boring
I hate the colour black.

Jennifer Keers (13)
Bangor High School

LOVE

Love is bright red
Love tastes like sweet tomatoes
It smells like fresh flowers
Looks like big red hearts
Love sounds like joy and fun
Love is happiness.

Karolyn Walker (12)
Bangor High School

MY MUM

My mum is the best mum you will ever find,
I'm so glad she is mine,
She cleans my room and washes my clothes and she also cooks,
And when I went to Bangor High, she helped me pack my books.
When I'm down she cheers me up,
By bringing me tea in my favourite cup.
When she closes my door at night,
In the morning she makes me feel nice and bright.
But that's my mum, the best in the world,
And she is very glad I'm her little girl.

Carly Huddleston (12)
Bangor High School

HAPPINESS

Happiness is yellow
It tastes like lemonade
And smells of flowers
It looks like Ronan Keating
And sounds like Boyzone
Happiness is wonderful.

Christina Ackerman (12)
Bangor High School

BIRDS

Nervous
Chirping with excitement
Ready to fly
No wings!

Suzanne Morrow (13)
Bangor High School

LEAVING

Told we are leaving
Shocked by the news
Upset and angry
Why?

Told we are leaving
I hate them,
They make me mad
I feel sad.

Told we are leaving
I'm hollow inside
Leaving my friends
And relatives behind.

Told we are leaving
Starting a new school
New teachers, new friends
Everything will be new.

Told we are leaving
Don't want to go
Not now, not ever,
Not going, *no!*

Andrea McDowell (12)
Bangor High School

THE OLD WOMEN

I know an old woman who lives in a cottage
and is all alone.
I go up to see her every now and then
and she is quite happy, she's my gran!

Rachel Orr (11)
Bangor High School

LOVE AT FIRST SIGHT

Day hot and depressing
Room filled with people,
Shouting and discussing,
Too much to handle.

I get to the end of the room,
There he is.
I can feel my body burning
I am going to melt,
Like an ice-cream on a hot summer's day.

All becomes silent.

You can hear a pin drop,
My world has stopped and now,
Revolves around him.

He winked
Such beautiful eyes,
The picture has been captured.

I never believed in,
Love at first sight,
Until now.

Eleanor Green (15)
Bangor High School

THE TEDDY BEAR

My mum bought me a teddy bear
My sister took it everywhere
I cried and cried until I got it back
My, oh my, thank goodness for that.

Emma Monroe (12)
Bangor High School

AUTUMN

Blow wind blow
Swirling and whirling
Waving branches
Blow wind blow
Whistling, singing
Gusty and rushing
Blow wind blow
Orange leaves rustling
Branches swaying
Blow wind blow
Crispy and crunching
Autumn it must be
Blow wind blow.

Susan Thomson (13)
Bangor High School

SMOKING!

People smoke in depression
They smoke in anger too
Little do they know what is really happening to them
They loose the redness in their cheeks
Their health goes down the drain
Their teeth and tongue and fingernails go a yellow colour
They may get cancer or something else
All they're really doing is killing themselves
They take five minutes off their life with every one they smoke
Then before they know it
They're in their lonely graves
All because of those stupid
Packets of cigarettes.

Mary-Louise Williamson (12)
Bangor High School

LOVE

Love is here,
        all around us,
Love is heartache,
        love is clear,
Love is real,
        love is always,
Love is forever,
        love is fear,
Love is pleasure,
        love is pain,
Love is eternal,
        love is insane,
Love is a picture
        that dwells in our hearts,
Love is a link,
        which can't be torn apart.

Gemma Ward (15)
Bangor High School

TEACHERS

Teachers are funny,
But sometimes strict,
They like to give homework;
But usually we forget,
We do the right homework,
Without even knowing,
And usually get marks we'll never forget.
Teachers also admit when they're wrong
I think that is why,
I've liked them so long.

Gemma Logan (12)
Bangor High School

SPIDERS

Spiders are hairy
Spiders are black
Spiders are scary
Especially in the dark.

Some are big
Some are small
Some don't even
Bother at all!

But when you see one
You begin to scream
But after all, they are
Not as bad as they
Seem!

Tracey McCamley (13)
Bangor High School

LIFE

Life is hard work
Exhausting, boring
Too many hours in a day.

But on the other hand
It can be fun, exciting, brilliant.

Life can also be sad,
Happy, lots of prospects.

Life is full of heartbreak,
Crying, new babies being born,
People getting married.

Lynsey Campbell (12)
Bangor High School

OLD PEOPLE

We see obsolescence as something we do not look to.
Hours lingering slowly without a task to do.
Unending days, sometimes they seem all alone.
Warmth and protection not much of that they own.

No friends left to keep them company,
Only a fire to keep them warm.
They sit lonely and tired, sheltering from the storm.

They sit there still as a crumbling statue,
With nothing to do but look right at you.
In their eyes, you see their sadness,
In their decaying bodies, their anger, memories and
Their madness.

Lying there lifeless with their final breath gone,
But with every sunset there is always a dawn.

Kelly O'Corrain (14)
Bangor High School

THE TIGER

The tiger is king of beasts
All animals bow down
They are his loyal servants
That is until we come along.

If he fights us, we fight back
We have ruined his land
We have killed him
Only animals have respect
For the tiger anymore.

Erica Harmar (14)
Bangor High School

THE SKY AT NIGHT

The sky at night,
Is like a dark blanket,
Blocking out the sun,
With tiny white polka dots,
Shining, sparkling,
Some are big,
Some are small,
Some even shoot across the sky,
Like a long lizard,
There's also the moon,
All different colours and tones,
Making a shape of a face,
Looking, staring,
Just at you,
Nobody else,
The sky at night.

Heather Craig (12)
Bangor High School

JAMES BOND

J   ames Bond
A   lways kills his enemies
M urderers and gangsters
E   ver ready
S   ecret agent.

B   ig and strong
0   07
N   ever
D   ies.

Alan Beggs (12)
Bangor High School

THE BIRD

The dawn of time arrives for the chick.
It opens its eyes and is finally awake.
The chick attempts to fly, to put its life at stake.
As it dives down to the ground, it opens up its wings.
It is flying, soaring through the sky in great joy it sings.
Finally it stops for a rest on a tree branch so high.
It is hungry, it needs some food, so again it takes to the sky.

After a good day of life the bird is tired,
It builds a nest, and sleeps.
The morning arrives and it is such a lovely morning
That the bird sings like a choir.
A week later the bird is sitting in its nest so happy, but why?
As the bird rose from its nest it revealed an egg
And then took to the sky.
The bird came back with food and another life began.

Holly McKee (11)
Bangor High School

SCHOOL

English, maths, science
Work, work, work
I really hate school
Pupils should rule.

School is tiring
Six hours, five days a week
When you get home
You've a pile of homework
That's why I look forward
To the weekend.

Chris McAllen (13)
Bangor High School

HALLOWE'EN NIGHT!

Little children dressed as vampires
People set alight the bonfires.
Fireworks go *bang!*
Bangers explode,
There are witches, bats
And spotty green toads!
There are toffee apples,
Sparklers
There are also ghouls and ghosts.
The toffee apples have to be
What I love the most!
It may make you jump with fear,
It may make you jump with fright.
But it's always so much fun
Every Hallowe'en night!

Emma Shaw (13)
Bangor High School

TRUE LOVE

True love is like a blooming rose,
My love for you just grows and grows.
It is as enchanting as a summer's day,
It is fantasy like a Shakespearean play.
Love falls on you like drops of rain,
Love gives you pleasure, love gives you pain.
My love for you is real and blind,
My love for you is cruel and kind.
But my love, I must attest,
That true love really is the best.

Lucy Pragnell (14)
Bangor High School

IF I WAS . . .

If I was a millionaire,
I'd spend and spend and spend.

If I was a famous actress,
I'd perform in the Grand Opera House.

If I was a gorgeous model,
I'd boast my Calvin Klein.

If I was an athlete,
I'd run to Timbuktu.

If I was a Prime Minister,
I'd stop the world from war

And if I was a poet . . .
I'd write a poem like this.

Jennifer Warden (13)
Bangor High School

AUTUMN

The leaves are falling from the trees,
Turning into golden leaves.
They're crisp and delicate and very fragile,
They dance about so incredibly agile,
They glide around like soft and
Sophisticated butterflies.

When the children come out to play,
It's sure the leaves won't see another day,
The crunching and crackling sounds so much fun,
But the leaves just wish autumn had never begun.

Susan Crozier (13)
Bangor High School

LONESOME AND AFRAID

She sat in the corner, lonesome and afraid
Her hair like spider's legs, thin and scraggly
I can see her ribs piercing through her skin when she changes
For PE, like needles through a pin cushion.
It is easy to see she isn't as fortunate as me.
Should I ask her to hang out,
Or should I leave her in her dark corner, lonesome and afraid?
I wonder how her parents react when they see her with a new friend?
Do they shout? Do they hit her?
A year later she isn't lonesome or afraid, she has me!
Her parents are so kind, so what was the problem before?
It is cancer! But at least she knows I am here to support her
And we will get through it together.
She will never have to be lonesome or afraid again,
She will always have me no matter what!

Linzi White (14)
Bangor High School

HATE

Why have happiness when you can have hate?
When you have someone that you hate,
What he says and what he does
Will never change the way he was.

Sharing, caring and loving too,
Why bother if it's not about you?

This hate inside me is eating away,
Like a disease, it will finally destroy me,
Unless I can find a cure.

Zoe McMullan (14)
Bangor High School

MY DREAM TEAM

I've loved football ever since I was seven
I've always dreamt of a special team
A team of eleven players and a stadium
And this is my team.

First I would have Peter Schmeichel in goal
Then I would have Maldini, Keane, Stam and Viera
In midfield I would have Beckham, Redknapp and Bergkamp
And Marc Overmars
And strikers Alan Shearer and Ronaldo

The stadium would have to be Wembley
The team would be called International FC
The coach would have to be Sir Alex Ferguson
And I would be making millions.

Chris Burns (12)
Bangor High School

MY FAVOURITE PLACE

My favourite place is the sweet shop,
I love it with a passion.
I go there nearly every day,
In sun or wind or when it's lashing.
Cola bottles, 10p mix, rhubarb rock and Cadbury's Twirl,
Caramel, Maltesers, brandy balls and Walnut Whirl,
Midget gems and cherry lips,
Polo mints and strawberry whips.
The only time I really pout
Is when all my money has run out!

Christine Gibson (12)
Bangor High School

FAMILIES

They are always there for you
And help you when you're down.
But when you need some understanding
They drive you up the wall.

With Mum telling you not to be late
And Dad asleep in the corner,
You're just about to go out the door
When you argue with your brother.

Sometimes you just can't stand them
And others you get along fine.
But to tell you the truth
You'd be lost without them.

Suzanne Morrow (13)
Bangor High School

LOVE

Love is a special feeling.
Like a fire in your heart.
When you see that person
Your heart beats
Your stomach flutters
Your head spins.

Love is fantastic but love is cruel
Love is the solid sand when two people fall in love
Love is the drifting sea as love comes to an end
Your heart breaks
Your stomach turns cold
Your head comes back down to Earth.

Karen Walker (15)
Bangor High School

BLESS OUR SCHOOL

Our school may not be perfect,
but it is glorious in God's sight.
The students may be rough and bad,
often soft like a dove's feather.
The teacher may be tough and tight,
but some may be as soft as leather.
Some students may be shy and lonely,
but they have always got somebody there.
Other students may be nasty and smart,
but they are the ones who spoil the peace.
The school may look like an evil jail,
but in some ways it is a joyful happy mansion.
So I pray to you Lord please . . .
bless our school.

Kirsty Meredith (11)
Bangor High School

LEAVING

Leaving
my house
my friends
my teachers
my neighbours
my school
my bedroom
my garden
my uniform.
Why?
How could they?

Cherie McCracken (12)
Bangor High School

LOVING YOU

I thought we'd last forever
and always be together.
I never wanted it to end
and I hope my heart will sometime mend.
You broke my heart in two
and it's all because of you.
We had our good times and our bad
and it makes me feel so very sad.
If I had a wish, I know what it would be
it would be something for you and me.
My love for you will never die
as long as you don't make me cry.
You told me you loved me and I thought it was true
all the love I have is just for you.

Elaine Mills (15)
Bangor High School

WRONG WAY ROUND

If it was the wrong way round,
Or things were up instead of down,
A smile would soon become a frown,
A cat would land on its back,
The coal would be around the sack
And then pigs could really fly
And cows would float in the sky.
What if dogs could talk
And sharks could walk!
I guess I'm glad that it's this way,
Or I'm afraid I'd have to say,
I'd be in more dismay every day!

Teri Robinson (13)
Bangor High School

HALLOWE'EN

Ghosts, spooks, witches, monsters,
Scary stories, scary sightings,
Pumpkin heads that move,
And lanterns that flash.

Children trick or treating from door to door,
Teeth marks in apples,
Toffee dripping and chocolate,
Leaving a trail to somewhere unknown.

In a graveyard the skeletons arise,
As the walk of the skeletons starts,
The ghosts come out and scare the living,
While I just dream.

Hannah McGrady (11)
Bangor High School

MY WISH

Half my life I have wished for a horse
With a coat as black as ebony
And its mane shining like a
Shimmering black diamond.

Its only marking would be a snow-white
Star in the middle of his beautiful forehead,
Causing eyes to stare at his beauty.

This would be my horse
More precious than gold
And it is my wish
That I will always hold.

Judith Reid (13)
Bangor High School

THE WINTER SNOW

This morning I looked out of my window
And saw cotton wool buds drifting down
I thought very hard about what had happened
The world had been attacked by a giant sheet of snow
The air felt very cold and chilly
The world looked so pure and clean
I ran out through my front door
And touched the soft silkiness of the snow.
There are footprints from the postman
Up my garden path
And children playing and building snowmen
The world looks so different with the snow on the ground
The snow will melt and go away
But in our minds the joy will stay.

Sarah McIntyre (13)
Bangor High School

AN ELEPHANT

Squirt, spurt, squirt
Splish, splash, splish
As the elephant shoots water from his trunk
Swish, swash, swish
Whoosh, swhoosh, whoosh,
As he swings his long grey trunk from side to side
Thud, thump, thud,
Clump, clomp, clump
As he thunders along the ground with his huge feet
I know he's big and could trample you flat
And then you would look like a big squashed hat!

Tina Mackey (12)
Bangor High School

ALIENS

Aliens, do they really exist?
Do they zap up cows and people
Take them half way across the
Universe without a blooming clue?

Did they drop us on this planet
To watch like in a zoo?
Or are they just like us looking
Into the unknown?

Are they intelligent? Do they have six arms?
Where do they live?
Do they live here, do they live there?
Aliens, do they really exist?

Ryan McKenna (12)
Bangor High School

HALLOWE'EN

Witches on their broomsticks
It's that time of year again
When the ghosts and ghouls fly
Straight over the round moon.
They land on Earth just for the night
And make up spells just to spite.
It's Hallowe'en and the night is dim and dark,
The frightened screams of children can be heard,
Fireworks dive through the air,
But witches, well they don't care,
As they weave in and out between,
Their silhouettes, whoosh.

Melissa Moore (13)
Bangor High School

LOVE!

Love is happy,
Love is blind,
Love takes over the whole of your mind!

You can't think straight,
Your love's rivals you hate,
Love can come soon and love can come late!

Love is cuddly,
Love is warm,
But also in love your heart can be torn!

So, beware of love,
As it's sent from above,
And always look after the one that you love!

Victoria Couch (13)
Bangor High School

LOTTERY

Waiting on a Saturday night,
To see if you have won.
The tension rising in our heads,
Wondering if, we are going to be the one.
The balls come out,
You check your ticket,
And think to yourself,
'This is really wicked!'
Have I got four or have I got five?
Even the bonus ball.
I take a second glance and notice . . .
I've got none at all!

Suzanne Patterson (13)
Bangor High School

WITCHES

There was an old woman
With warts and sties
With hair on her chin
And two crossed eyes

Me and my dog
Went to her house
And to our surprise
She was eating a mouse

Then we ran away
And left her alone
With her warts and her sties
The cross-eyed crone.

Emma Sloan (13)
Bangor High School

LOVE AT FIRST SIGHT

Love at first sight,
Cupid takes his first bite.
Suddenly struck, standing so tall and still,
Your whole world stops, your heart begins to fill.
Your legs are soft, they turn to jelly,
Your heart tumbles over and over in your belly.
Your eyes are sharp, you can't seem to blink,
Your head is messed up, you can't seem to think.
This guy is sweet, he looks so fine,
I wish we were a couple, I wish he was all mine.
We could travel the world, north, south, east and west,
Just me and that guy, because he is simply the best.

Louise Withers (14)
Bangor High School

BUBBLES

Bubbles, bubbles everywhere
Floating gently in the air
Reflecting colours like a mirror
Children run happily as they try to
Catch the beautiful, soft bubbles,
As they climb higher
The children faster
Until
Pop!

Megan Williams (12)
Bangor High School

STEPS

S uper
T alking
E xercising
P op group
S inging.

Sarah Dundee (12)
Bangor High School

ANGER

Anger is when you are really down
Anger is when someone makes up lies about you
Anger makes you feel so down
Anger feels like the end of the world
I hate anger!

Lauren Waddell (13)
Bangor High School

THE WRONG TIME

That lad fancies a girl I know!
I didn't think that was possible,
The way he stares,
The way she glares!
I felt like I shouldn't have been there,
Her nice blonde hair,
His smooth ways,
Hmm . . . I wonder if I hadn't have been there,
Then maybe fate would have had its day.

Barbara Garrett (15)
Bangor High School

BABIES

B ig and bold
A lways alert
B ouncing off furniture
I   nterested in everything
E ating like monsters
S ilently sleeping.

Kirsty Beattie (14)
Bangor High School

SUMMER

Summer is bright yellow
It tastes like green apples
And smells of flowers
It sounds like birds singing
Summer makes me feel happy.

Zoe Douglas (13)
Bangor High School

LURKING IN MIDNIGHT WATERS

Her hair quivers like cool reefs
Her skin is as smooth as tears
And deep in the pools of two diamond eyes
Lurk the secrets of a thousand years

Her scales shimmer like oyster pearls
Her mind, as unpredictable as the sea
Fins as glossy as the swaying seaweed
With the name of Tonyalee

A heart as warm as the Caribbean
Yet never completely free
But under the midnight waters
Wanders beautiful Tonyalee.

Jennifer O'Neill (14)
Bangor High School

WHY?

Why are you doing this,
When will we leave,
What about my friends,
Where are we going?

I don't want to go,
I hate you!
How could you do this to me,
I'm not going!

What about this house,
What about my school
What if there are bullies?

David Glover (11)
Bangor High School

LOVE POEM

One day I saw this handsome face,
I fell into his warm embrace.

His open arms so warm, so tight,
Never did I feel love so right
And at that moment I hoped and prayed,
'Please let this moment never end,'
But sure enough it came to pass
And sadness gripped me as we moved away.

All I could do was think of him,
Hoping that the day would pass,
So we could see each other again at last
And so the day passed and at last,
We both met up to recover the past.

Caroline Gibson (14)
Bangor High School

MY FRIENDS

The things I couldn't live without are:
My friends!
My friends are the best,
Of course they're silly and insane
But they're there for me when I need a laugh
Or I'm feeling down.

My friends, I do everything with them.
We shop,
We swim,
We eat,
And we even muck around together,
And that's why we have each other!

Lynsey McCullough (11)
Bangor High School

TEACHERS

T eachers are terrifying
  E very lesson is boring
    A fter school detention
      C lasses last too long
        H our by hour I look at the clock
          E very teacher is the same
            R eady to yell all the time
              S chool, I wish it never existed.

Kelly Hamilton (13)
Bangor High School

FRIENDS

Friends are always there for you,
Even when you're feeling blue.
Boys may come and boys may go,
But friends will be there to help your through.
Friends will be with you until the end,
You can always rely on your friends.

Natalie Cranston (13)
Bangor High School

FRIENDS

Friends are always there for you
And will never turn away from you
They are curious and kind
They're hard to find
And I know that I've got my friends
By my side.

Natalie Lightbody (12)
Bangor High School

STARS

Stars like diamonds shine
Far up in the Milky Way
Gleaming light, ever twinkling
Like an avenue of day
Far, oh so far away
Beyond our reach
Bright, sparkling dazzling array.

Jemma McClure (13)
Bangor High School

JOY

Joy is pink,
It tastes like strawberry milkshake,
It smells like a meadow of flowers,
It looks like a fluffy cloud,
It sounds like happy children,
It feels like a cat by the fire.

Lee-Ann Hamilton (12)
Bangor High School

HAPPY!

I am happy having fun
Happy at the beach
Happy with people around me
Happy when I'm playing
Happy that I'm young
Happy to be me.

Kirsty Mulholland (13)
Bangor High School

MOVING HOUSE

I'm shocked
    sad
      angry
      empty

leaving my pets
      friends
      school

Moving house, why?
         When?
         How long?
         What area?

I hate them, I'm not going!

Stewart Lemon (12)
Bangor High School

PEACE!

I love my mum
I love my dad
I want everyone to be on my side.

About peace in the world
All fighting to stop
I want there to be no need
For armies or a cop.

If only everybody saw
Things my way
The world would be a better place
Every single day.

Debbie Smyth (13)
Bangor High School

ALCATRAZ

I walked silently, the gravel crunching under my feet.
It loomed into view and sat there grinning in the shadows.

I looked back at the steel gates,
at least six feet high, securely bolted and locked,
the one that was open was guarded by a hefty looking man.

My shoes clicked in the silent halls
that lead towards 'the dungeon'
where the prison officer would be waiting.

I opened the old wooden door and crept quietly to my seat.
Unfortunately the executioner spotted me and yelled
'Late to school again! Detention for you!'

Hannah Bell (14)
Bangor High School

SNOWMEN

Snowmen are round, funny and fat,
They have a carrot for a nose,
And a big floppy hat.

They're white like clouds,
And cold to touch,
But never seem to stay around too much.

They have eyes like night,
With a grin to match,
So why not try and give him a fright.

Karen Verner (14)
Bangor High School

MOVING HOUSE

Disgusted, mad, angry
How could they not tell me

Furious, shocked, upset
We're moving away from everyone I know

New house, new street, new friends
We're moving away from them all

New school, new teachers, new mates
Hoping it won't be so bad.

Kara Lutton (11)
Bangor High School

THE TIGER

Miss, there's a tiger in our classroom,
It's gobbling up my classwork book,
Its teeth are like twenty kitchen knives, sharp and pointed,
Its tail is long and curled like my sister's curls,
Its eyes are like oil lamps, bright and burning,
Miss, if you believe me,
Please help, I think I'm for dessert!

Helen McDermid (12)
Bangor High School

AUTUMN

Autumn is the season
When leaves fall off the trees
All the children running round
In the gentle autumn breeze.

Summer's gone
Autumn's come
Running through leaves
Is so much fun.

Cheryl Moore (13)
Bangor High School

THE MOVE

How dare they?
Why?
Let down
New school
New friends
New house
Let down
Lonely
Moving house.

Christopher Marks (11)
Bangor High School

EVACUEE

E motions spread throughout the train station
V iolence was on the way
A nxious children boarded the cold trains
C restfallen parents waved goodbye
U nable to believe their children had to go
E ndless tears ran down children's faces
E very child was an evacuee.

Emma Gallaher (13)
Bangor High School

LOVE

Love is bright red
The taste of spaghetti bolognese
Smells like chips
Looks like a bunch of red roses
Sounds like Ronan Keating
Feels like floating through cushions of clouds.
Love is happy!

Samantha Clint (13)
Bangor High School

ANGER

Anger is a dark red
The taste of hot chilli
Anger smells like smoke from a fire
It looks like a massive bonfire
On Hallowe'en night.
It sounds like a wicked laugh
Anger feels like a stab in the back!

Grace Nicholl (13)
Bangor High School

THE BIRD

I am a bird that can soar through the sky,
You may have seen me glide gracefully by,
I am a bird with silky white wings,
And when we are preened we are the prettiest things,
I am a bird that is pretty and bright,
You really must see me . . .
What a beautiful sight!

Karen McCulloch (12)
Bangor High School

BROTHERS

Young, old, fat or thin,
Some are bright and some are dim.

Some have glasses, others a brace
Some wear trousers, that are a disgrace.

Brothers are brothers, come what may,
My brother's my friend, at the end of the day.

Stuart Young (11)
Bangor High School

THE DOVE

As white as snow
The dove does fly
With its silver wings
Gracefully in the sky
Back home to its nest
Home to its little ones
Peacefully to rest.

Tara Lindsay (13)
Bangor High School

ANGER

Anger is dark blue
It tastes like sour milk
And smells like rotten eggs
Anger looks like a dark forest
It sounds like people stepping on dried leaves
Anger annoys me.

Esther Magee (12)
Bangor High School

FOOTBALL

F un to play, fun to watch
O utrageous decisions by the ref
O n and off the players go
T railing behind at half time
B rilliant teams like Liverpool playing
A lways winning to teams like Newcastle United!
L eaving their fans wanting more. At
L east there is always next week.

Elizabeth Weir (14)
Bangor High School

TEACHERS

T eachers are real nice.
E very teacher has a classroom.
A t ten o'clock the teacher said.
'C ome to me, let's read a book.
H ow are you doing?' she said to me.
E very teacher has lots of books.
'R obert,' she said 'come to me.'
S ee teachers are really nice.

Dawn Hughes (12)
Bangor High School

TIME

Time is never ending
It's part of night and day
It's like a flowing stream
In its own continuing way

Over time things change
Like the world that changes every day
Time is never ending
Like memories that always stay.

Judith Reaney (13)
Bangor High School

SCOTLAND

S cotland
C aptivating
O ld clans and
T artans
L ively
A nd
N ever
D ull!

Ryan McDowell
Bangor High School

LEAVING HOME

Leaving
When?
Why did they?
How dare they?
I wonder
I do not want to go
I hate them
Leaving.

Andrew McNabb (11)
Bangor High School

THE SHARK

The shark
Hunting through the water's depth
Wide eyes as he sees his catch
Mysteriously he turns sidewards
And then propels himself through the water at top speed
Rising a little to the surface
His fin slices and separates the rippling water
His prey has been lost
And won to another.

Sara Watson (12)
Bangor High School

LOVE

Love is beautiful,
Love is kind,
Love is sweet,
It's always on my mind.

Love laughs,
Love cries,
Love breaks,
It reddens your eyes.

Kelly Hinds (12)
Bangor High School

SHOES

Shoes are so wonderful
They always make me smile.
They cheer me up when I am down,
They pick me up from the ground.

Shoes are my life, my friend
And my hobby.
I love shoes so very much
They make me feel so funny.

Stacy-Leigh Neill (12)
Bangor High School

HALLOWE'EN

H allowe'en
A ll alone
L ight the candles
L ight the torches
O ff we go, come a noise
W itches and wizards
E ach on a flight
E cho from the
N ight.

Ryan Lee
Bangor High School

HALLOWE'EN

Hallowe'en is full of fright
All the witches look a sight
Hear them spit, cry and scream
These are sounds of Hallowe'en

When I'm lying in my bed
Broomsticks whizzing overhead
Was it real or did I dream?
Did I hear the witches scream?

Clare McCann (14)
Bangor High School

THOUGHTS OF AN EVACUEE

Instead of laughter I am now a burden,
I have tags hanging on my neck and my suitcase,
Like an early Christmas present I head for the station,
Not yet ready to leave my family,
I clutch tightly to my suitcase,
It is filled with familiar things,
My memories of home.

I board the train unwillingly,
The children are silent and scared,
With tears in my eyes, I find a seat,
I sit there all alone,
For what seems like a lifetime,
Then the train bangs to a sudden stop,
The stop that I had been dreading.

The billeting officer is standing straight and tall,
Her face is unfriendly and scary,
Her eyes are blue, like ice,
Her nose long and pointy like a mouse,
She lines us up in order of height,
While adults choose which of us to take.

Farmers are picking tall, strong boys to round up cattle,
Women are picking girls that can sew,
Older people are picking the smallest, quietest ones,
I am left standing on this platform alone.
There is no one here for me.
Just then I get tapped on the shoulder,
An old woman is looking down at me,
Her kind, warm eyes a welcoming sight,
She is opening her arms to me.

Ashleigh Kennedy (13)
Bangor High School

THE HAUNTED HOUSE

Down deep in the middle of the forest
There stands a haunted house.
Nobody dares to enter
Not even the bravest florist.
It creeks and howls in the windiest nights,
It even falls apart,
The kind of night that blows away the washing line.
Look, there's Granny's tights.
To get in, there's a big black door,
That reaches 160 feet.
One man's started to climb it,
He should be there by the next world war.
When inside you get a shock,
Cobwebs and rats galore.
Out comes Lurch, the big, scary butler,
Who grabs you in a headlock.
Once you pass him, if you can,
You enter the twilight zone,
With ghosts and vamps everywhere.
You better hope to see the Scooby can,
Puppy power!
After the zombies, you're almost free,
Knowing you, you'll trip.
Oh, no, the exit's stuck,
Well don't look at me.
So you've been here forever, how does it feel?
I hope you've learnt your lesson.
When you see a spooky house,
Don't go in . . .
Never.

Lyndsey Pentland (12)
Bangor High School

OLD AGE

I sit alone,
Hoping my family will phone,
My husband is dead
I sit alone, full of dread
They put me in this stupid home
To sit all day, all alone
They barely come here
Only about once a year!
I am like an animal in a cage
And why? Because of old age!

The days drag by
As I wonder why
My husband was taken away from me
I used to be so happy
I am like a prisoner
All I need is one visitor
Patiently waiting for that person to come
Lying here, acting dumb
Lazily lying here all day
Watching people drifting away
As I sit here sipping my tea
Looking over at the person opposite me
We are all animals in this cage
And all because of old age!

Sarah Turley (14)
Bangor High School

RETIREMENT BLUES

Old age is a time most people dread
Not knowing what lies ahead
Will they be lonely and cold
Or will their friendships hold?
Will they start wearing tweed jackets and a cap
Or will they still wear jeans and a baseball cap?

Old age is like a piece of string
You don't know how long it will be
Some people may cruise into the sunset
Of their golden years
Others spend time alone in tears

Everyday tasks become much longer
As old people's limbs are not as strong
Purple rinsed, permed pensioners
Their teeth not their own
Waltz round the tea dances
Then go home alone

Monday mornings bring delight
Pensions got
Cream buns for tea tonight
The rest of the week falls into place
Continuing their journey
Through life's long maze.

Lynsey Beatty (15)
Bangor High School

DAY AND NIGHT IN HEAVEN

As dreams end,
The day starts,
The ocean of golden granules, shimmer in the rising fire.
The tranquil desert is broken by the calling of tropical birds awakening.
The day is beginning.

The burning ball of fire, hangs high in the sky,
The intense heat bakes the exposed desert.
The parched creatures search the barren water holes,
And then the storm begins.

The wind rises,
Burning sand grains like a golden rippling ocean.
The sand storm spirals,
Then as if vanishing, it stops.
Its coiling tentacles fade away,
As darkness sets in.
The desert has turned to night.

As the mistress of midnight forms over the land,
The lights of heaven shine through the coat of darkness.
The moon reflects on the dark desert sand,
Casting uneven shadows on the vast wilderness.
The desert sleeps.

As first light breaks,
The creatures of the night retire to their peaceful slumber.
Then the deserted desert is again, full of life.
Where animals roam its everlasting expanse,
And another day has emerged.

Samantha Murphy (14)
Bangor High School

MY PET GUINEA PIG

I have a little guinea pig
Dasher is his name.
Sometimes I feed it fresh fig
To make it very tame.

It lives in the garden shed,
That is where I keep his bed,
And that is where he is fed.

Henry James Abernethy (11)
Beechlawn School

FIREWORKS

Mum and Dad took us out.
In the park we walked about.
Fireworks made sparks
Sparks in the dark.
Sparks fly up in the sky,
As the rockets fly high.

David Curry (11)
Beechlawn School

MY PET

I wish I had a little pet.
A dog it would have to be.
Brown and yellow I would get.
These are colours I like to see.
Miss Piggy, I would give for a name.
We would try to have a game.

Fiona O'Neill (11)
Beechlawn School

MY PET DOG

I have a little dog
And I call him Fog.
He likes to play and catch the ball
In our garden, it is small.
He is very big and black.
I got him in a little sack.
One day my dog was very lame,
My daddy gave me all the blame.
We had to take him to the vet.
Now he has his back leg set.

Seaneen McLaughlin (11)
Beechlawn School

MY PET MOUSE

My pet mouse
Lives in a little house.
He plays on his little wheel
And goes round and round a great deal.
He goes zoom, zoom, zoom
Up to my bedroom.
I love to watch him everyday
In my bedroom as I stay,
And sometimes we would play.

Jonathan Bell (11)
Beechlawn School

MY PETS

I have a dog, her name is Cassie,
She is a sheepdog, just like Lassie.
Cassie is always chasing her friend,
On that I really can depend.

I have a cat and her name is Korky,
She is very fat and a bit porky.
She loves to sit on my lap,
Sometimes she curls up in my dad's cap!

Jennifer Graham (11)
Beechlawn School

HARRY HAMSTER

Harry Hamster is my pet
But I had to take him to the vet.
Poor old Harry is very sick
Because his fur was not too thick.
He is white with little brown socks
And he lives in a cardboard box.
It's my job to give him feeds
I do everything he needs.

Andrew Irwin (11)
Beechlawn School

WITHIN THE TROUBLES

Oh why have the tides of fate turned on me,
That I should love a loathed enemy
That my mind should conceive like this,
When within my grasp is total bliss.
And do I put myself to shame,
For a creed, a past, I have to blame,
Does an angel as fair as she
Deserve a fallen wretch like me?

Conor Holmes (16)
Campbell College

2000 THE MILLENNIUM

The millennium, a big celebration
people going out
people sitting in
it's our game, move it all about.

The millennium, a big celebration
music blaring
people staring
I can't get to sleep because people are scary.

The millennium, a big celebration
more acceleration
cars crash, cars bang
it's all right
if you have a Ford Mustang.

Steven Beers
Down Academy

THE YEAR 2000

The millennium is near
At the end of this year
Just around the bend
Our thoughts will lend
We will all have such fun

As the century unfolds
We will visit other worlds
Our brains will expand
To meet the demand
Of better health
And greatly increased wealth

My sister's birthday is on that day
Although it is not
Really far away
I cannot wait
Because of the great date
We'll boogy the day away.

Suzanne Hobday
Down Academy

THE FUTURE!

The world is spinning,
And technology is changing.
Oh to witness such a scene.
That not even my great, great grandchildren will see.
I hope to interact with my TV
And have the computer play with me!

Andrew Houston (11)
Down Academy

2099

In the year 2099,
What will become of all mankind?
Will we walk to the nearest shop
Or just press a button,
And up it will pop.

Will mankind wear clothes?
Or even space suits.

Will kids stay at home?
With no more school, or press another button
And a teacher will say 'Now listen up kids
Here's your lesson for today.'

No more cars, buses or trucks
We'll all go about in a space shuttle.

Will we be on Earth, or even Mars?
No more cafes, graveyards or bars,
'Cause who's to say we'll be here at all.

For 2099
Is a far away call.

Roseanne Johnston
Down Academy

I HAVE A DREAM

I have a dream in a few months' time,
With the twentieth century at the end of its time,
That all of the world will not have to beware,
That the Millennium Bug is only a scare.

To some it is a time to fear,
For others it is another day of the year,
When important decisions must be made,
To me it's the start of another decade.

To live in harmony and silence sustain,
The guns and bombs never to hear again,
A time to remember things of the past,
To look forward for peace in the world to last.

Tornadoes and hurricanes have battered our planet,
Leaving death and destruction for everyone in it,
The future for mankind is not as bad as it may seem,
I will always remember that I have a dream.

Mark Andrews (11)
Down Academy

THE MILLENNIUM

I have a dream
That when the millennium comes
That there will be world peace

I have a dream
That when the millennium comes
There will be no starvation and poverty

I have a dream
That when the millennium comes
People will be judged by what's inside them and not
By their religion and skin colour

I have a dream
That when the millennium comes
Everybody is rich

I have a dream
That when the millennium comes
Dreams will come true.

These are my dreams.

Amy Murray (12)
Down Academy

2000 AND BEYOND

2000 and beyond
we know not what will be
with flying cars
and trips to Mars
oh what fun it will be.

Sitting in bars
watching shooting stars
while drinking champagne
and feeling no pain
oh what fun it will be.

Men from Mars
in silver cars
whizzing through space
with amazing grace
oh what fun it will be.

Sitting in bed
with thoughts in my head
the future approaching
soon dawn will be breaking
oh what fun it will be.

Sara Price
Down Academy

MILLENNIUM

If I could wish upon a star
My millennium dream would be a new car,
For my mum and dad they do so much,
For my wee sister she would just wish
For just about everything.

If I could wish upon a star
I would wish to be a famous pop star
Like Sporty and Mel B
I would just have to wait and see.

Sarah Carlile (11)
Down Academy

MILLENNIUM

In my perfect new millennium,
I want to see,
People like you,
And people like me,
Living together in perfect peace.

No wars between colours,
No wars between creeds,
No wars over lands,
No wars over seas,
Living together in perfect peace.

Animals for the pleasure to see,
Not for the fur in the fashion industry,
Yes we need animals for food,
But keeping them housed with some dignity,
Living together in perfect peace.

Let's hope for the future,
From the old millennium,
We can learn from mistakes,
And make some improvements,
And hope for,
Living together in perfect peace!

Lynda McSpadden (11)
Down Academy

CHANGES FOR THE MILLENNIUM

Don't be cruel to the animals,
they haven't done anything to you,
why can't you just go and visit them,
while they're playing happily in the zoo?

Don't be cruel to the whales,
they only want to swim in the sea,
can't you just be thoughtful,
and let them be *free!*

Don't be cruel to the tigers,
just let them be free!
They only want to live happily
with their families.

So please don't be cruel to the animals,
they do no harm to you,
just go and watch them,
live happily in the zoo.

Holly Douthwaite (11)
Down Academy

FUTURE

F uture plans for the New Year's Eve,
U tter excitement, 2000 brings,
T ime is changing, the bug is here,
U nfolding secrets will make it all clear,
R evealing the plans that everyone's made,
E njoy the treats and party atmosphere.

Anna Smith (11)
Down Academy

MILLENNIUM

I sit and write this poem
and the future looks quite bright,
we'll see tourists going to the moon
now that would be a sight.

I look into the future
the road is full of cars,
perhaps we'll all be flying,
could the next stop be Mars?

We'll celebrate with style
we'll welcome the new year,
it's the millennium 2000
we'll toast the future
with great cheer.

Sarah Smith (11)
Down Academy

THE YEAR 2000 AND BEYOND

Will we still live in houses?
Will we still go to school
In about 20 years?
Will people be any safer on the roads?
Will we still get around on cars or
Some new invention?
Will the clothes we wear change
Or will we wear recycled materials?
What will become of us?
Nobody knows.

Tanya Hamilton (11)
Down Academy

MILLENNIUM POEM

I had a dream -
of lands of plenty,
freedom and justice
no wars, just peace.

I had a dream -
no work, just play
fun and pleasure
all the day.

I had a dream -
a happy, carefree dream
if I waken -
will it be reality?

Daniel Mills (11)
Down Academy

THE FUTURE AND BEYOND

In the future there will be new things
There are cars that float
New animals
New life forms
Maybe there will be aliens
Maybe there won't
Maybe there will be robots
Maybe there won't
Maybe there will be time machines
Maybe there won't
Maybe, maybe, just how maybe.

Ross Breen (12)
Down Academy

IN THE YEAR 2000

In the year 2000,
Will we still have to go to school,
Can we still go to the chippy,
Like we used to do?

In the year 2000,
Will there still be hungry people?
Will countries still be fighting,
In the year in which to come?

Will anybody know these questions
Which I would like answers to?
Maybe if we try together,
These things might just come true.

Jane Thomas
Down Academy

WE'LL HAVE TO WAIT

As 12 o'clock comes, I stand and wait,
Will this be the end of life?
Will the world end tonight?
If not will my watch stop?
My video not work, my computer crash?
Will planes fall from the sky?
Will our dishwasher flood our house?
Should I go out or just stay in?
I just don't know what to do
But I do know one thing,
We will all just have to wait and see.

Ryan Douglas (12)
Down Academy

I HAVE A DREAM

I have a dream that one day there will be peace in Northern Ireland
I have a dream that one day there will be peace in the world.

I wish that everyone would get on with one another
And fighting will end.
I wish that one day I could play football for Northern Ireland
And save a penalty in the World Cup.

It does not matter if you are black or white
It does not matter if you are Protestant or Catholic.

I have a dream that one day all my dreams and wishes will come true.

Michael Thomson (11)
Down Academy

MILLENNIUM POEM

M ichael is one of my father's names
I   myself am called James,
L ooking forward to seeing Mum,
L ight our bonfire for the millennium,
E verybody in our family will stay up late,
N ephews and
N ieces, brothers and sisters,
I   know I just can't wait to help,
U lster celebrate with the world, the new
M illennium.

James Gordon (11)
Down Academy

SHE'S STILL MY FAVOURITE OLDER PERSON

When somebody says
Who's my favourite old person
I think of Paddy.
She's not related to me
But that doesn't matter.
She's still my favourite old person.

When I see her she gives me hugs
Not the tiny ones, big ones
Like big bear hugs.
She listens to my problems,
Play games with me when I'm bored
And she laughs when I make jokes.
She's still my favourite old person.

When I'm walking down the street
She doesn't embarrass me.
She doesn't spit on a hanky
And wipe my face like other grannies.
But I don't mind
She's still my favourite old person.

When I think that one day she might die
It makes me very sad.
I would miss her a great deal
But I know that she will be okay
And I still know
She's still my favourite old person.

Alanna Kerr (14)
Glenlola Collegiate School

NATURE

A cat has a coat
Like a lion
All tabby, stripy and brown
A dog is a person
In a way
The way it moans and groans
And cries if left alone.

Shells swim and swirl
In the sea
And also stick to rocks
Like the way
Glue sticks to paper
And Blu-tac to a wall.

Emma Morris (12)
Glenlola Collegiate School

THE SPACE WE SHARE - REQUIREMENTS

Peace and understanding would meet the requirements,
Love and freedom would satisfy the whim,
Wisdom and strength would make a completion.
All is possible if together relationships come,
Come into the presence of one another
In the hope each aura will combine.

A combination of love and peace will gratify
Understanding with freedom
In return the strength will be satisfied
And wisdom will finally be complete!

Gemma Loughlin (16)
Glenlola Collegiate School

THE DEATH OF DAY

The death of day
The night has just began
The evil and the surreal light
Plagues the doorway and the hall
They have arrived . . .
They're not really here
They bring that noise
That deadly silence
Will they not keep quiet?
That hum infests my would-be sleep
The night is fading now
The people are leaving
The light peeps through the curtains
Unreal light goes away
Shadow and reality merge
I'll go to sleep now.

Janine Brown (18)
Glenlola Collegiate School

BUBBLES

When you blow through the stick,
The little baby bubbles are born.
They gently soar through the air,
Like tiny aeroplanes,
Yellow, red, green and blue,
Brightly shine through them.
As their journey comes to an end,
They float gently towards the ground.
Like an eagle to its perch,
And pop like tiny bombs.

Stephanie McFarland (12)
Glenlola Collegiate School

TREE OF LIFE

The gnarled old tree
Cultivated in the living room.
By the fire, the armchair stood
In this sat the well-dressed,
Gnarled tree
With waves of white glossy hair.
Until the day he had a stroke of bad luck
Then the gnarled old tree could bear no leaves
The armchair in the living room was then unleafed.

This was the end of one life
But another had just begun.
It was pink
A shrivelled up prune.
He lay still,
Twined in twigs.
The twigs soon broke,
When the prune developed
The branches grew
And the leaves stretched.
This was the beginning of his life.

The old year has died
And lost its leaves,
Bearing only the seed
To create the new.
The New Year
A new life
Growing from the seed of the old.
The new will spring great things.

Just like the peacefulness and the joy
From the birth
This joyful year,
Will soon be born.

Dale Maginnes (14)
Glenlola Collegiate School

OUR PLACE

As we move through life
The world is ever changing.
People of different races
Joining together
To become united.

Hidden secrets
Revealing themselves
Small, tall, fat, thin.
People brought together
Through love
Shapes, colours, curves and straights.

Never-ending love,
Sad times, difficulties.
Overcome in a never-ending maze.
Family and friends bring us together.

Honesty, secrets, excitement, happiness.
No one is alone if they have love.
When people leave the heartbreak and suffering,
They turn to find friends,
In this peaceful place.

Keri Connolly (16)
Glenlola Collegiate School

MEMORIES OF A GOODBYE

Deep pretty blue eyes that once shone bright like pearls
Above rosy red lips that whispered, 'we were her girls'.
On creamy soft skin with a few cracks and flaws.
'Simply cleanse, tone and moisturise,' these were her laws!

Long, curly, white locks framed this delicate face.
They were always a mess, a total disgrace!
But she never cared, curls hung wild down her back,
She had such a free spirit, something I lack.

Her bubbly personality - oh boy!
The only tears she cried were tears of joy,
And her warped sense of humour and the jokes that were old,
They just weren't funny but we laughed at the way they were told.

Her fragile body clothed head to toe in something she'd knit
Based with grey, fur-lined walking boots, she liked to keep fit.
It's now clothed in a gown made of satin or silk,
The colour of her skin, pearly like milk.
And these pretty blue eyes now shut out the light,
And the rosy red lips have turned pale - it's not right!

Then she disappeared as the coffin lid was sealed,
And her beloved husband wept as he kneeled.
We'd never see her again so we tried to be strong.
But that's not quite true because her memory lives on.

Claire Long (14)
Glenlola Collegiate School

MY CAT

He slowly opens his green eyes
And licks his black and white paw
Then gently lifts and rotates it round his ear
Before he gracefully jumps off his comfy chair

He walks round my legs
And brushes his fur on my ankles
Then turns on the floor, laps up his milk
And goes back to sleep.

Laura McIlmurray (13)
Glenlola Collegiate School

LEARN FROM THE EXPERIENCED

The sky is such a marvel
Billions of beings,
Never fighting,
Slowly evolving,
Each shining.
Doing what it does best.
New ones born, old ones die.
The sky mourns and celebrates,
And lives in peace.
Are these pinpricks we see,
Letting light shine through from above?
Are these sparkles in the sky,
Begging us to stop,
And look at ourselves?
Look at how pathetic we're being?
How irrelevant all this bickering is.
Stop.
Just stop, please,
And listen to them,
We might learn something
From their years of experience.
They might share some with us,
And teach us how to live.

Catherine Bell (15)
Glenlola Collegiate School

MAN, I CALL MY OWN

Not far away in a land unknown,
Lives a man I called my own.
His hands as big as elephant ears,
And skin as dark as lions,
But not long ago this man I know
Was called Grampa Joe.

He lived his life as no other did,
Telling secrets of love, life and knowledge.
His eyes told a story of years gone past,
And his mouth never frowned
With the day going by.

Grampa Joe held those special keys
To wisdom and magical things.
Never telling that secret to even his wife
Hiding his fears away.

Not far away in a land not known
Lives that man I called my own.

Claire MacDonald (14)
Glenlola Collegiate School

OUR SPACE IN LIFE
(For my best friend C B)

As time goes on, as seasons change
the way we are remains the same,
the space we share, the love we feel
never unnatural, never unreal.

The people we know, the people who care,
it's with those we give our space to share.
To have the company of them by our side
never changed with wind or tide.

As we grow old, situations change.
Love's always there widening its range.
The people we've met, the people we've known
will all have differed, matured and grown.

Among these people, family and friends,
there's someone special. Who? Depends.
With them your life will lengthen and grow,
your space, your happiness only you will know.

Laura Murray (15)
Glenlola Collegiate School

MERRY MILLENNIUM

I hope the future holds better times.
This past year has held tears, disappointments and a few laughs,
For our community and as well for the whole country.
There has been the Good Friday agreement,
Many peace talks.
But it has also seen things
Like the Omagh bomb and
Many serious punishment beatings.
I hope the year 2000
Will hold peace for Northern Ireland.
Which would be some consolation
For all those people who have lost friends
Or relatives in the 'Troubles'.
I hope it would also bring
A few personal successes
So Merry Millennium.

Jenny McIlhatton (14)
Glenlola Collegiate School

Diary Of A Virus

23.30 - 00.00
Still dark outside
When I opened my eyes
My pillow wet
Damp with sweat
The mirror shines
And the only light
Is the reflection
From the hall lamp
That Mum leaves on.

00.01 - 03.30
Too tired
Too sleepy to care
Too restless to sleep
Pains in my tummy
An ache in my head
Tired and weary
'Mummy!'

03.31 - 07.00
Medicine and tablets
Flocks of sheep
First hot
Then cold
Then boiling
Then freezing.

07.01 - 09.00
No sleep yet
And no school today
The first alarm's ringing
The first shower's going
Still tired, restless, weak, weary
The breakfast dishes rattling.

12.00
Asleep now
The cleaning lady . . .
Trying hard to be quiet
Daytime television on low volume
Better.

17.30
Teatime
Not hungry
More medicine
More tablets
More sleep.

08.00
Birds singing
Bells ringing
A better day
A better face
Still white
But alright
The virus is gone
On to it's next victim.

Megan Gray (12)
Glenlola Collegiate School

A LOSS OF LOVE

Her wrinkled, aged skin,
Her twinkling sapphire eyes,
Fun and loving,
Kind and wise.

Hours pass by,
I listen, she talks,
Of summers gone,
And windswept walks.

Flirting at dances,
Theatres and plays,
The fun never ended,
In the good old days.

We search through old photos,
I see a strange man,
And down her thin cheek,
A single tear ran.

Shaking her head,
The tear flew away,
The sadness is gone,
And the smiles will stay.

She tells me a tale,
Of the man that she lost,
In the Second World War,
Her heartbreak, the cost.

Her lips curving upwards,
A smile in her voice,
She tells me of all men,
He was probably last choice.

But at the back of her heart,
There's a sad memory,
Of his face as he left her,
While she sat on his knee.

She touches her lips,
Recalls their last, goodbye kiss,
And the look on her face,
Is momentary bliss.

She's much too stubborn,
To let her sadness show,
It'll make them downhearted,
Nobody should know.

She visits his grave,
To feel that he's near,
And cloaks her grief,
In a semblance of cheer.

I think she's special,
And soon you'll agree,
Old people are special,
To you and to me.

Karen McKee (12)
Glenlola Collegiate School

THIS WORLD

There are many people in this world
all from different parts.
We all may be different,
but we've all the same heart.

We all must share the space between us,
no matter how hard it may seem.
We should all make space for each other,
living in unity as a team.

We must try to combine together
as like friends or family.
Residing in close-knit communities
held together by peace and harmony.

We really aren't so different,
we have more to unite than divide.
With our hair colour, skin colour and size
we have emotional feelings inside.

Each heart, it holds its own pain and sorrows
each eye mirrors the hurt of each soul.
How can we inflict pain on each other?
As there is already enough to unfold.

It costs nothing to exchange a smile
and yet it means so much.
The effect of that simple gesture
can transform the people we touch.

Linda Coulter (16)
Glenlola Collegiate School

HERITAGE

I am ashamed of you again, of what you are, of what you claim to be,
I'm a part of you - yet so distant and unconnected that it seems unreal
You ask me to wear your colours but I don't understand
                              what they mean,
How can I love what I hate and hate what is my own?
The young man that lies dead in the gutter is fury from your heart,
The burning wrath of three hundred years still ripening the
                              seeds of hate,
I watched the children playing just before the blast,
And I felt love and I saw peace - and you took it away again.

You claim to be a soldier but for what country do you fight?
To satisfy a sickening streak you maim the innocent,
Is this soil worth the red shed blood that stains it through and through?
Why do you glorify the pain you cause or treat this as a war?
Tell me what you're fighting for, why you hold your head so high,
Why I must fight and I must die, to save this tainted land?
The politicians lie to us, they say that there is peace,
Then I've seen your weary dead get up and walk and turn
                              within their graves.

The orange flags are flying to match green, white and gold,
One step forward, two steps back, the lies have all been told,
I do not like my heritage, you make me so ashamed,
Your cause unjust, you do not care, your hate it can't be tamed,
You live in fear of a peaceful day and then what will you do?
'Cause nobody likes a killer, a radical just like you.

Catriona Holmes (16)
Glenlola Collegiate School

87

A SPACE OF MY OWN

I hear the crashing of the waves,
and the wind blows through my hair,
I think there is someone behind me,
I turn around - there is no one there.

I am all alone,
yet the feeling is there,
I can feel others' presence,
yet I don't even care.

As the wind blows strong,
my hair's being curled,
it's my own little seat,
in my own little world.

I think of the others,
I think of my friends,
deep in my own world,
thoughts I will send.

People say I'm crazy,
people say I'm mad,
but this is my own space,
surely, it's not that bad.

As I sit on the pier,
in my own little seat,
different people I see,
different thoughts will I meet.

I don't care what people say,
but that place is my own,
it's my own little world,
that no one else has known.

J Monson (15)
Glenlola Collegiate School

MEMORIES

Long lives with distant yet clear memories,
stories to be told,
to be enjoyed from generation to generation,
secrets kept as secrets,
no bright shining key could ever unlock those tales,
yet in all of this,
something special,
that has to be earned
appears from the mist-memories.

People don't change with age,
yes, their ageing bodies slow,
but at the heart, the life,
they don't change
they just grow:
older and wiser
in appearance and knowledge.

Older people are often generalised,
although I know truth lies elsewhere,
my grannies are different,
and my grandpas too,
well what can I say.

It annoys me, when the younger generations,
forget the facts
older people were here before us,
so they deserve respect, everyone has their turn
at being younger then older,
but it all depends,
on how we live our lives,
whether we will be wiser or bolder.

Jane McDowell (14)
Glenlola Collegiate School

MILLENNIUM

My past was interesting
Like a vase of flowers, all different,
Some good, some not so good.
A lot of times were terrific.
Times I will never forget,
But others, just some others,
Were ones that I hope
Will never happen again.

Birthdays, Christmases, family and friends,
Losing my first teeth,
Memorable, happy times were those,
But times come that change happiness,
Like giving away my first pets,
And some other times
Were cruel, hard, unhappy moments,
When life seemed like a bitter lemon.
Those times that cropped up were difficult,
Those times that were hard,
Chunks of my life that I don't want to happen,
Ever again.

The year 2000 sounds really good.
I wonder if I really should
Be happy about it, well why not?
It's a once in a lifetime lucky jackpot
To see the new millennium.
All the excitement makes me go numb.
The new and improved games and toys
For all the good girls and boys.
Big fast cars and fancy fashion.
No more wars and nothing to ration.

All we have to do is be patient
And wait for peace to conquer all
Every person, big and small.
That's my hope for years to come.
A happy world for everyone.

Elizabeth Patterson (12)
Glenlola Collegiate School

WHEN I WAS A CHILD

When I was a child,
I used to cry.
Sit in the corner,
and look into the sky.
I would watch the stars,
as they shone above,
and wish I could be free,
free as a dove.
But things have all changed now,
there is no time to sit and stare.
There is work to be done,
with no time to spare.
There are exams to revise for,
and chores to be done.
There is no time to have,
lots of fun.
The millennium is coming,
it's time for a change,
to stop all the wars,
and lock up the rage.

Emma Hanna (15)
Glenlola Collegiate School

THE GATHERING

Trains carry us to the spot,
Businessmen are roused from their mobiles
By decadent, glitter-splashed halogens
That fill the carriages.

We descend up it with the masses,
An Edwardian hall, suddenly transformed.
People who don't belong, who live the cliché,
Suddenly we're old friends,
This hall, our old meeting point.
A fixed date,
Like a personal ad, we all respond, all attend.
The freak show has come to town.

The huge oak door opens and inside, a lonely hall,
Like an anti-church, we congregate there.
When the eyes turn to the stage
There is no such thing as me.
There is just the sweeping carpet of bodies,
People floating on top, seemingly dislocated arms.

The encore ends, the lights come up,
For a second, it shocks, thrust back into reality.
The flying carpet settles into another hall,
Crushed plastic cups replace people,
Glitter and sparkling stars catch the light,
Drowned in sweat and washed off into the arena.

On the train, with ripped skirts and panda eyes,
The nameless conversations recommence,
More sweat-embalmed faces to recognise,
More stories to hear and tell.
Enjoy the company - it's fleeting
The train carries us away,
Back to normal routine, normal obscurity.

Until the next time.

Beth Rodgers (17)
Glenlola Collegiate School

MY GRANNY

My favourite older person, has to be,
Well, of course, it's my granny you see.
Her coloured glasses, her white hair,
Oh what would I do if she weren't there?

She hums her songs as she bakes,
Her lovely voice, it helps the cakes.
She bakes her scones and her bread,
And all these recipes come right from her head.
They taste so good, I love them so,
Oh, what would I do if she were to go?

She loves her 'soaps' 'specially Coronation Street,
She just sits back and puts up her feet.
She loves her cups of tea,
'Specially if they're made by me.

My granny is special,
And I love her so.
Oh, what would I do if she were to go?

Jane Noble (13)
Glenlola Collegiate School

THE LYON NEXT DOOR

My new next-door neighbour - the Lyon next door,
Is a wrinkly little old lady, eighty-three or ninety-four?
When greeting people she says 'Hello!
I'm Mrs Lyons, as in the zoo!'
But although she puts on this brave face, I know she's lonesome too.
Whoever heard of a wrinkly lion, well Lyon is her name,
And as for wrinkly, she certainly is that, but I like her all the same!
A gardener to do her gardening and a cleaner to clean!
A friendly friend to natter with, what a lucky old bean!
Always watching through the window, she waves as I stroll by:
Although I know she can't hear me, I quietly call out, 'Hi!'
I know she's small and wrinkled with nooks and crannies too,
She's always full of stories, (I believe not a word is true!)

Sarah McVeigh (13)
Glenlola Collegiate School

THE GROWTH OF TIME

The face of time
Has not yet grown,
It lies in a barren place.
Where oceans of topaz and rubies grow.
Calcium is drawn to the bone.
With growth and swelling
Comes structure and strength.
The beginning has ended
Endings have begun.
The race hasn't started
But the hands still run.

Sonya Moorhead (17)
Glenlola Collegiate School

94

ANOTHER WORLD

The sea is a person,
with all her own friends.
A totally different world
from ours.
The people who own it,
are the fish that swim about.
The plants are seaweed,
and the houses are cracks
and 'caves' in the rocks
below the surface of the sea.

But I live in my world
and they live in theirs -
another world.

Victoria Nelson (12)
Glenlola Collegiate School

MR MAGEE

There is a man called Mr Magee,
He lives down the street from me.
Some people say he is strange and shy,
And that he wouldn't hurt a fly.

He is big and strong just like a bear,
His head is covered with curly brown hair.
If he growled you would run a mile,
But most days he would just give you a smile.

So if you should meet Mr Magee,
I wonder what you would see.
A gentle man all meek and mild,
Or a roaring bear about to go wild.

Kathryn McNair (12)
Glenlola Collegiate School

In Exile From Evolution

Mother and child, equally beautiful.
Born of a virgin, the child inherits its grace through true love.
It is the sweet song of the blessed child
which heralds their presence as one.
As man engraves time's name on mother's rock of rest,
he can only be humiliated by his frantic labour,
for like the sun and the moon,
it is the strength of their beauty which can determine the seasons,
casting shadows on the livelihood of a pagan, a stamp for his doom.

While the world sleeps, mother offers her secrets to the child
she bore of divine nature. As she signals to the oyster the time to feed,
the eye of the bow glistens with pearly splendour.
As she sweeps through the woods of ebony, together they capture
the richness of maturity. And, as the birds glide through the air
in morning flight, they offer their music as a gift to mankind.
Then, when man's chains pull them back to the dusty quarry of time,
mother clings to her child. For where the nightingale
finds her inspiration, be the birthplace of the violin.

Joanne Elliott (18)
Glenlola Collegiate School

A Trip To Paradise

Fond memories of Tunisia
Play gently in my mind
Blue skies, turquoise sea
White sand that almost blinds.

Exotic spices in the souks
Camels plodding through the sand
All part of the dazzling paradise
That makes you feel happy in this land.

I soar above the coral reefs
Like an eagle as I paraglide
Thrilled, excited, nervous, free
A once in a lifetime ride.

My taste buds explode
As they try to deal with the delicious, unusual food
Roast lamb, shellfish, couscous stew
Paradise could never be so good!

Esther Kyle (15)
Glenlola Collegiate School

JUNKIE

You are my cocaine.
You release me of my pain.
You take away reality,
And cut my binding chains.
You support me while I grow;
Hold me - don't let go.
You understand my torture.
You let my spirit go.
You let my tears rain down
And tell me not to frown.
You take away my battered soul
And replace it with a crown.
You accept my truth and fiction.
Pour water on my friction.
You are my star,
My source of power.
Yes, you are my addiction.

Rachel Gibson (15)
Glenlola Collegiate School

THE SPACE WE SHARE

Nothing is out there,
No human life but ours.
Weird creatures perhaps.
White silvery bits of magical 'fairy dust'
Shine brightly from that open space.
We're not alone, we have many people
That we can relate to.
All different shapes, sizes and colours.

We need to be out there.
Exploring the space.
It seems so much fun.
Yet some of us feel the need to hold back.
The need to widen this space.

We should be drawn nearer
Into a new 'era'
We need to go exploring,
This big open space,
To close it together,
To rejoin it as one.

Laura Kirkpatrick (15)
Glenlola Collegiate School

THE CITY OF MONOPOLY

I went away with my family for the weekend,
To a city we all love.
We like to visit the sights and see
The city of monopoly.

When I went the first time
I was unaware of my surroundings.
I was afraid of getting swept with the crowds
And getting lost in this huge place.

But now I can't wait to return again,
To see different cultures and people
And to see all the shops and sights
For another time.

Lynne Chalmers (15)
Glenlola Collegiate School

OLD BUT YOUNG

Time matures the lines, pulls on her face.
It sets in her bones and stiffens her body.
Still when I gaze into her eyes, into her soul,
a softness lingers behind, always there,
especially in her smiles and frowns
that radiate the youth inside.
But soon enough that melts away,
revealing a less than able, thin and frail,
little old woman, a small, empty lady.
In her heart is locked a past,
deep to touch.
A broken heart no one could mend.
I respect her for all she is,
all she is to me, all she stands for.
However much we fear the deep onset of time,
the thought of wrinkles, thin hair and frailty,
with it comes knowledge of a well-led life.
The wisdom and maturity that can only be learnt
from a lifetime of experiences, good and bad.
We can't cheat our way to this infinite knowing.
Just wait for time to do its work,
knowing that one day her pride will be mine.

Helen Baker (15)
Glenlola Collegiate School

THE PASSAGE OF TIME

Every second dies
like a fly in an angry cook's kitchen.
Every hour passes
as quickly as the blink of a tired lion's eye.
Every day wanders away
like a lost boy in the woods.
Every week runs away
with night and day.
Every month dies
like 1000 daggers in the old cobbler's heart.
Every year trickles away
like blood on the bay.
Every decade escapes
like a jailbird out the window.
Every century passes
like a cat in the dog pound.
Every millennium
well we'll just have to wait and see.

Tracy Knox (14)
Glenlola Collegiate School

A TIME FOR CHANGE

In the past
there were bombings and terror
pain and sadness
death and murder.
We have suffered so much
but for what?
Hundreds of people have died
for no reason.
Fighting isn't solving anything.

The future reveals itself
as a time for change
a new beginning
a time to wipe the slates clean.
A time to forget about the past hardships and troubles
to blank out the bombings and terror.
A time for peace!

Allie McAuley (15)
Glenlola Collegiate School

DAY BY DAY

As I wonder about the future,
I start to think about my past,
I have so many memories, they will surely last.
In my mind I see thousands of colours, smells and feelings.
All so real, too real.
I feel a wave of sadness passing over me,
A feeling that however much I cling to them
Standing there an innocent little girl smiling
For the pictures that they took.
I never thought of the bad things,
Only the good.

But now it seems
Like my eyes are opening for the first time.
I now notice the bad things
Like death and crime.
People I love are slipping away,
So I live my life day by day.
Is there anyway out of this for us all?
The millennium is coming to call.

Gemma McAleer (14)
Glenlola Collegiate School

MY FAVOURITE OLDER PERSON - GRANDA

You're the only Granda I've got,
the only one I've ever known.
Without you I don't know what I'd do,
I'd be so alone.

I can remember when I was younger,
down to the beach we would go,
looking for muscles, cockles and willicks
to bring them home in a great white bucket.

We would boil them in salty water
and then we'd eat them with lots of vinegar.
I doubt if I could eat one now,
but then I had no trouble.

Everybody knows you,
and you're everybody's friend,
and even though your ways are stronger,
you're still a brilliant man.

I know I should visit you more,
come to see you and Granny.
It's no excuse for you to hear
but I've just been so busy.
Sorry.

Laura Girvan (15)
Glenlola Collegiate School

TRANSFORMED TO GOLD

The mountain air swept down on our play,
cool on our faces, hot from our fun.
The fields of grass transformed to gold,
by the streaming rays of the heavenly sun.

The days of play that seemed never ending,
up by the water that glistened so bright.
It's the place that I love, and for now and forever,
the memories of there I'll hold deep in my heart.

Katie Croan (15)
Glenlola Collegiate School

AMERICA!

My family's first holiday abroad, what an experience.
What a great day to go, the day of independence.
Jumbo jet all the way, taking off gave me a fright,
the feeling you get when your knuckles turn white.
There we were, the land of dreams, the big USA.
Disney Caribbean, that was the site of our stay.
Off we went sunbathing on the beach,
well at least I know this is one thing no school can teach.
Seaworld was great, especially the whales getting us wet.

International Drive, the place where my friend Alan and I met.

Travelling in high style on the fantastic shuttle buses,
and shopping around in the sales where everyone rushes.

Everyday parades with all the stars like Mickey Mouse
and Donald Duck.
On the last few nights of our holiday it rained, just my luck.

My holiday quickly drew to an end,
many letters that I promised to send.
Back home to Bangor where it always rains
and now I'm home, all I have is dreams to visit America
once again.

Jennifer McKnight (15)
Glenlola Collegiate School

MILLENNIUM

Born into a family with my mum, dad and two sisters,
taking my first steps and learning how to talk.
Toddling along the beach in France at the age of one,
crawling towards the sea before my dad could catch me.
Ouch! My finger! Caught in the door, my first major
accident at two years of age.
My first house move to Donaghadee.
Aaah! Hurtling round the track at 110km p/h
Eight 360° vertical loops,
hanging upside down in my safety harness.
Three minutes of the highest tension, that's Dragon Khan,
The largest rollercoaster in Europe!

Oh! All the fuss about another year,
all the 'I wishes' and 'I'll think of you my dear'.
The Millennium Dome, huh! What a waste!
People should have better taste!
I feel privileged in a way, to experience a new millennium.
It's not like there's plenty of 'em!
I hope the millennium will bring peace as it comes,
instead of leading people along by its side,
fighting and shooting each other with guns.
The millennium, me or my family,
the most it could do is help us live more happily!

Gemma McElroy (12)
Glenlola Collegiate School

THE ROUND

Life is like a circle
It just goes round and round
It feels as if I'm lost
Or being tightly bound.

When will I be set free?
When will I be found?
When will I escape
From the ever present round?

Joanna Little (14)
Glenlola Collegiate School

WHAT'S REALLY OUT THERE?

The air we breathe
Is space we share
Clean air, polluted air,
Warm air, cold air,
We share it all.
We share with humans, birds and animals
Do we share with aliens?
Who knows? Perhaps we do!

The house we live in
Is space we share
Big houses, small houses,
Terraced houses, detached houses,
We share it all.
We share with family, pets and friends.
Do we share with ghosts?
Who knows? Perhaps we do!

We share our space with
Many different things.
Perhaps even UFOs and
Things that go bump in the night.
But, who really knows what
We share our space with!

Claire Goodwin (16)
Glenlola Collegiate School

REFORMED CHRISTIAN

I, Shylock, should be admired
For my courage
For persevering through the loss of a daughter
And the losing of my soul.

Do you Christians
Still want to laugh at me?
Mock, and spit on me?
Call me names?

If I were cowardly
I would not have had the courage
To seek revenge.

Do you still see me as a Jew
At heart?
Or a reformed Christian
Showing every likeness to you?

I showed courage in the courthouse
Though you squashed me
Like a fly
No mercy.

Like a wounded soldier
I cannot use my weapons
But I will revenge
I am a hero
I can endure.

Heather Johnston (15)
Glenlola Collegiate School

MY GRANDA

My favourite old person is seventy-two
He lives up in Belfast with Gran
Loves fishing and hunting and walking and more
He's surely the best of the clan

Although he is bald and walks with a stick
Has one finger missing and deaf
He still has his humour, his wit and his jokes
And sometimes can be quite a chef

He's fun to be with when he dances and sings
Though sometimes he just sits and reads
He is very thoughtful, kind-hearted and sweet
He also enjoys planting seeds

Lately my Granda has taken quite ill
Has been in hospital a lot
Some people say that he's not got long left
So we'll make the best of what we've got

Everyone's worried about the wee man
Though he's had a really good life
But all of a sudden, bedridden and ill
Everyone's going through strife

Hopefully Granda will be here a bit longer
As we all just love him to bits
He's a special, a funny and thoughtful wee man
And in our hearts always will fit.

Jenny McGarvey (14)
Glenlola Collegiate School

SENSES

Totally oblivious to people all around me,
I stand in the midst of beauty, listening.
The sweet song from the birds slowly whispers
Through the trees,
And the water gently cascades over the cliff's edge,
To join the rippling lake below.

The flowers in full bloom sway in the gentle breeze,
That rustles past the crisp green leaves on the trees.
A lone bird whistles a joyful tune,
While a shimmering fish leaps out of the clear,
Shivering water, almost as if to greet me.

This place is full of joy and beauty.
It's full of memories of good times too,
And it fills me full of happiness, when I think of it.
I love this place because,
It's a space we share.

Castlewellan.

Rebekah Lunn (14)
Glenlola Collegiate School

PLAYSCHOOL

Oh, take me back
To my childhood days,
Where things were so gay
And meeting up with friends again
And playing happily.

Oh those were the magical days,
Playing, dancing and painting.
Where we could do what we wanted
All day long,
And no one would say a thing.

Oh of course there were sad times,
When we would fight and cry,
But these were overcome with joy,
As we began to forget.

Oh I wish those days were here again,
I wish that joy would come.
If only I could dance and play
Like in our old playschool with all
My friends and the fun.

Catrina Graham (15)
Glenlola Collegiate School

THE GREAT OAK

Ah! There you are my long and trusted friend,
Why has no one looked after you while I've been gone?
You poor creature, you've been through a rough time.
Wind thrashes at you with painful blows,
You're long bony fingers reach out,
But no one answers.
Your poor old face creaks with every move.
People judge you foolishly by your stern face.
Pain strikes at you with every chance,
Taking great joy in knowing,
This old creature can't take anymore.
But inside your love and warmth is home to many
Tiny helpless creatures.
There is no one to help you,
Or listen to your long, sad, old story
When winter comes again.

Alison McKibben (13)
Glenlola Collegiate School

THE SPACE WE SHARE

We walk two alone, together in our silent noise.
No negative energies are pushed into our circles.
Our energy is not shared.

Free, wide, spacious
Curious yet our hearts feel glad
To hope for the glow we soon shall have.

Slowly, closing in
Circles are combining, mixing
Taking energy from our others.

White, clear, forming us towards
A rush, heart beats faster now
Loud music we faintly hear.

A glow around everyone
A bright explosion when we collide.
Sharing their glow yet willing to have.

Bumping, grinding
Music thumping
Dancing on the floor.
Energy guarding our ring.
Movement when others move
Tightly, squeezed in.

Sore and tired.
Late at night, early morning back to free
Wide, spacious, fresh currencies back to normal
Two alone yet again, with the memory of a night
Where the heart of a city was on a corner of our world.

Caroline Barr (15)
Glenlola Collegiate School

REVIVAL

A wandering heart,
An inquisitive mind,
A suspended soul
Which no longer can rhyme
A passage of solitude
Is but an arduous chore
And a glimpse of revival
Like a far distant shore.
The rarity of mystery
Leaves not a notion in the head
To take hold of any rapture
As it falls like lumps of lead.

But wait! Awakening is something quite surreal
As it tears through every hollow
Bringing rampant, raging fear
The start is quite a picture
As it reckons with the head
Which is lacking understanding
Towards this enigmatic trend.
Control it? Not an option
As the bubbles start to rise
Starting first from the toes
Until delighting weary eyes.

It grows until a climax
Which by now has been fulfilled
And as it contemplates departure leaving
Every sense in flight
This should reinforce the message
That to laugh is only right.

Carolyn McIlroy (17)
Glenlola Collegiate School

DEATH AND OTHER DREAMS

I know what a moth means
When a whole night is spent
Chasing after one.
A Morpheus moth,
With grey and silver mazes
In her wings,
Fluttering through black.

Could he not have sent her to me as a butterfly?
His sister in prettier shapes of purple and red,
Or yellow death-shaded wings instead?
Her sticky legs
And trembling body on my skin
Made me shudder.

So I followed her all night,
Through garden after garden of uncertainty,
And into the woods and under the soil,
Just in case I'd wiped
Some magic dust from
Death's wings.
I suppose the good thing was
That I never really caught her,
Although it would have been
So romantic.

Erin Halliday (17)
Glenlola Collegiate School

A WILD DAY

The horses silhouette against
The coloured sky, the only
Noise is the munching of
Grass. At any moment they
Could go wild at a drop of
Rain or the smallest noise.

As the day goes on, the
Horses shelter in the shade
From the sun. Soon grey clouds
Roll over the smiling sun and
Round plump raindrops fall from
The sky like heavy parcels.

The horses' ears prick up and then
Flatten down on their heads. They
Gallop faster and faster over the
hill, the rain chasing them like
A bird of prey. The wind is
Whirling now, tails and forelocks are
Dancing in the wind wanting to stay still.

After a while the rain stops, the wind
Dies down and the sun comes out
Again. The horses calm down and cry off
And wait for it to happen again.

Katie Parsons (12)
Glenlola Collegiate School

STAY

Stay, don't leave and go
Don't leave me here in this awful place
Please, don't let me get so low
Tears are streaming, staining my soft, cold face

You don't seem to understand
How my life is dependant on yours
You need to forever hold my hand
Whilst my love for you continually pours

The pain in my heart is so acute
I can't hide it, my eyes are too sad
My mind cannot think, I am mute
Please don't leave, stay: please Dad

Those little things you do every day
The light you bring into the world
The only thing I ask of you is, stay
Don't leave your little girl

You seem so able and confident
That everything will be okay
Your love for me meant
Your life must turn and go a different way

So Father all I ask of you
Is stay with life to give
And grant my only wish, please do
The wish for you to live.

Hannah Vincent (15)
Glenlola Collegiate School

MY KIND OF THING

Prickly holly, the cold, the smell of Christmas
The same every year.
It doesn't change
Or does it?
New Year isn't all that exciting
Christmas is my kind of thing.
Surprising presents, turkey dinner and family
Midnight's too late.
You have to be sleeping before that
I wonder will the millennium be different?
I can't even spell it, never mind think about celebrating it.
What's so special?
Everyone's older, the world might end,
Different people think different things.
There won't be a long line of Roman numerals
Just MM nothing more, plain, simple MM
It probably won't be the end of the world
Maybe the start
The start of a new era
Changing for the best
No guns, no bombs, no weapons whatsoever
Just a nice, peaceful world,
We can all live in peace,
No fear, just peace
We can all trust each other
Maybe this millennium our technology will increase
Maybe we'll go to the moon on holiday
You never know!

Kellie McAlonan (15)
Glenlola Collegiate School

DETERMINED

It feels like pushing hard,
Against a very firm wall,
Trying to push it over.
Willing yourself to succeed,
Willing yourself to keep going,
Willing yourself to be first.

But in the back of my mind,
I think why should I have to do this?
I can't push it over,
I can't succeed,
I can't keep going,
I can't be first.

Then suddenly a piece of the
Wall falls off and you think
I'm determined to be first!
And you keep going until that
Wall has all been knocked down
And you have *succeeded!*

Becky Armitage (15)
Glenlola Collegiate School

MOTHER AND CHILD

Everyone has felt this connection once,
Sharing everything with their mother.
What she hears, you hear,
What she eats, you eat,
What she fears, you fear.
You share her hands, her eyes, her feet.

She gives up her life,
But she doesn't care.
Only one thing matters to her,
The place the two of you share.

Her body is yours,
Till the day you are born.
But on this day, I'm sad to say,
The link is sometimes torn.

Christine Long (14)
Glenlola Collegiate School

MY BEACH

As I walk upon this soft golden ground,
I can't hear a whisper, not a sound.
I'm all alone, but I don't care,
I feel the wind gently toss my hair.
On through this golden dust I roam,
Full of peace,
As if at home.

And as I walk, a shell I see,
Beautifully shaped, just waiting for me.
I bend down low to sweep it off the shore
Then look around to see if there's more.
And as I hold it to my chest,
I realise it's different from the rest.

It looks so perfect, not a flaw or crack,
It restores the faith I come to lack.
I look around at nature in glory,
Even this shell has its own story.
So I stay a while upon the shore,
Until ready to face life once more.

Sharon Long (14)
Glenlola Collegiate School

A LONELY DOG

I wish someone would tell me
What it is I've done wrong;
Why do I have to stay chained up
And be left alone so long?

They seemed so glad to have me
When I came here as a pup;
There were so many things we'd do
Whilst I was growing up.

The dad said he'd train me
As a companion and a friend;
The mum said she'd never fear
To be left alone again.

The kids said they'd feed me
And brush me every day;
They'd play with me and walk me
If I would only 'stay'.

But now, the dad 'hasn't time'
The mum says 'I shed'
She doesn't want me in the house
Not even to be fed.

The kids never walk me
They always say 'not now . . .'
I wish that I could please them
Won't someone tell me how?

All I have you see, is love
I wish they would explain
Why they said they wanted mine
Then left it on a chain.

Louise McCloy (15)
Glenlola Collegiate School

THE SAND WE SHARE

Running wild, free as a bird,
Mum's complaining, she thinks it's absurd
'Covered in sand, that's what you'll be'
I don't care as I head for the sea.

She sits in the car to await my return.
But I've still got lots of energy to burn.
I tear through the ocean, not a moment to spare
Mum's in a daydream, she no longer does care.

The middle of winter, I must be mad
When I get back to the car my life will be had.
Up to my waist in the waves full of foam
While the fish and the crabs are beginning to roam.

Time to get out now, time to go home
But no, not yet, I've still got to roam.
Across the beach, with enormous strides
Up to the sand dunes where I'm able to hide.

Puffing and panting I reach them at last,
And duck behind bushes as a family walks past.
Mum's looking now, she sees me, oh no
I guess that that means we'll have to go.

Into the car, the engine's turned on,
Oh no, the car has got stuck and the shovel has gone.
The sea's fast approaching, what will Mum do?
I quietly sit emptying sand from my shoe.

At last we're pushed free with help from a man
Who has been watching our efforts from behind in a van.
With sand on the car and sand in my hair,
Sand in my clothes, there's sand everywhere.

Julie Loyal (15)
Glenlola Collegiate School

THE SEA AND ME

When we went on holiday
we rented out a boat.
My mum would not get in it
she was worried it wouldn't float.
So we were on our way
we saw some lovely fish.
We saw a big blue shark
as pretty as you could wish.
I stared in wide-eyed wonder
when we came to a little island.
I sat and began to ponder
why the island had no sand.
Then my dad and co got out
and I told them just go on
I just wanted to hang about
and listen to the blue sea's song.
Then I was alone at last
looking down on the deep blue sea,
and then I was so happy,
it was just the sea and me.

Melanie Montgomery (12)
Glenlola Collegiate School

STAY BEAUTIFUL

How I love to be adored
I clasp my hands so tight
As if one move could prevent me from holding on
Now failure is a glory
I receive only to lose
But the silent message of the moment
Forever echoes inside my soul
Stay beautiful

Life is lost forever
Tomorrow is long gone
The crumpled heap upon the floor
Is me
Alone

As before the vivid image returns
Graces time where I thought there was no more
Gives me one reason to grasp at thin air
Hope is one thing to look for

Stay beautiful.

Keira Oram (16)
Glenlola Collegiate School

EXPRESS YOURSELF

If you feel happy, smile.
If you feel sad, cry.
If you feel the whole world's gone wrong
Just scream
Don't bottle it up,
Express yourself!

If your best friend is sad, comfort her.
If she's just won a prize, be happy for her.
If you want to give it all up,
Just cry.
Don't bottle it up,
Express yourself!

If you're over the moon, jump up high.
If you've just heard something funny, laugh real loud.
If the whole world loves you, be grateful,
Just smile.
Don't bottle it up,
Express yourself!

No matter what you feel,
Happy, sad, grateful, jealous,
Just remember one small thing.
Don't bottle it up,
Express yourself!

Christina Kennedy (14)
Glenlola Collegiate School

FIREWORKS

Fireworks are so colourful and bright,
I love to watch them at night
They fill me with excitement
Because they are so fun.
They are all different, each and every one.
Some are big and some are small,
But I just love them all.
As Hallowe'en draws near
More and more seem to appear.
Red, yellow, blue and green
Are the favourite colours I've seen
As they race up in the sky
They remind me of life and how it goes by.

Rachel Armstrong (12)
Regent House School

JOHN

Why is John late for his big interview?
Failed alarm, traffic jam, a car breakdown?
No, he took the train from Reading Station
To be sure of reaching London on time.

He read his notes while others chatted, slept,
Scanned the morning newspapers, looked around.
Workers, shoppers, hopefuls, ordinary folk,
But none of them arrived at Paddington.

In a split second, signal 109,
At 8.03am all was to change.
Sudden carnage, screams, burning, anguish, death,
Many cars unclaimed and phones unanswered.

Michael Houston (13)
Regent House School

THE SNAKE WAR

He wrapped his body around me,
Looking into my eyes,
He tightened his stance,
His breath was like rotten pies.

After a while, what seemed like an hour,
I couldn't feel my feet,
In the middle of nowhere,
I couldn't stick the heat.

I tried to scream,
But my voice wouldn't come out,
The snake wouldn't let go,
I had lost the bout.

I saw the snake open his mouth,
I saw his massive fangs, his mouth opening and closing like a peg,
His mouth got closer to me by the second,
He bit me in the leg.

After seven lethal injections,
I started to feel faint,
Now I wonder what I said,
To deserve to be *dead!*

Keith Savage (12)
Regent House School

GOBLINS

Goblins are creatures huge and fierce,
With their teeth your skin they will pierce.
With their claws they will rip you apart,
Eating everything except your heart.
With your heart they will gallop back,
To save it for a midnight snack.

The goblins are very scary creatures,
With their big, bulging, frightening features.
With their enormous feet they will tread on you,
It is certainly not the worst thing they do.
So next time you're walking alone in the wood,
Take a torch, I know I would.

Cara Glover (13)
Regent House School

THE CAT

The cat
is all shapes
and sizes
so mischievous
and slick

The cat
loves to
sleep in front of a fire
jump up walls
and catch mice

The cat
hates the look
of dogs
and loves the
comfort of someone's lap

The cat is
a woman's
best friend
as a dog is
to a man.

Sarah Conway (13)
Regent House School

THE OLD PARK BENCH

I sit alone beneath the trees
Weary walkers visit me
Some are pleasant, some are not
Some don't really care if I rot.

I sit alone, calm and still
I have never moved and never will
I am always here for those in need
And those who want to sit and read.

I have been sitting here for a long time
And by now have lost my glossy shine
People come and people go
Where they go, I'll never know.

I sit all on my own in the dark
For I am just a lonely bench in the park
I have lots of time to think about why
Some people stop, but others fly by.

Vicki Duncan (13)
Regent House School

DONAGHADEE

The town I live in is Donaghadee,
A lovely town surrounded by sea.
We have a harbour with two piers,
That's been here for years and years.

The lighthouse stands proudly with its light,
Beaming on and off through the night.
Keeping boats and ships safe at sea,
So their cargo can reach the quay.

The commons is a place to play,
Where children like to come and stay.
With swings and slides they play all day,
And never ever have to pay.

On the sea-front is the paddling pool,
Where the water is always rather cool.
Old pensioners also come to sit,
And watch time pass bit by bit.

Jason Waugh (13)
Regent House School

DARKNESS

It is black and motionless
At night it's there
You can be sure
I can feel it speechless

It is cold
It reminds me of
A wild creature waiting
For its prey

It's creepy and spooky
It's there for a reason
I don't know what
It's like mist or fog -
Lingering, floating

It's sad and lonely
It causes danger
It can be frightening
It's all together amazing
It's *darkness.*

Naomi McCorkell (13)
Regent House School

MY ROOM

My room is quite a small room,
But it can get quite untidy.
In one corner is my bed,
In another is my chest of drawers,
On top of this is my bookcase,
Beside of which is my wardrobe.

On the far side of my room,
Is my desk unit.
It contains my fold-out desk,
And places for all my books.
On top of this I keep my old school books,
Along with my radio.

In the darkest corner of my room,
I keep all of my other stuff,
Piled in two big crates with boxes on top of these.

And that's my poem on my room,
I hope you enjoyed reading it.

Richard McGuckin (14)
Regent House School

PORTAFERRY, CO DOWN

My favourite stroll is along the shore
Sparkling, blue waters and rocking boats
Come alive to my eyes.
Across the water is Strangford
To and fro the ferry travels
On the hour and on the half hour
From Portaferry to Strangford and back again.

Up the hill there's a windmill
Surrounded by the roaming of cattle
Munching on the luscious, green grass.
On Monday morning the journey begins
For nineteen miles we chase the lough
All that lies ahead is a six hour day of school
Then again I travel home
Back to our home town of Portaferry.

Claire McMullan (13)
Regent House School

THE SUN!

The circle in the sky that shines all day,
It gives earth light, every day.
It shines there like a light,
But where does it go during the night?
The moon is there, but not the sun.
But in the morning the sun rises high,
And the bright white moon disappears.

What if the sun runs out of fuel,
And doesn't shine anymore?
We will have no natural heat or light,
That will give us a real big fright.
When we had the total eclipse,
It went very dark and cold.
Just imagine it being dark, day and night.

But as everyone knows,
The sun will not burn out,
Not for a few millions years or so,
So it will not affect *us* much!

Wayne McCully (13)
Regent House School

THE HAMSTER

The hamster chews on his cage every night
And makes me lose my sleep
He shuffles around and makes lots of noise
And doesn't care about anything

He is a Syrian hamster who is golden brown
His fur is as soft as wool
He is friendly and playful
And likes to eat treats

He destroys everything he sees
Puts holes in curtains
And pulls up the carpet
And he bites you if you try to lift him

He is so smart, he's learnt so many tricks
He can climb up the stairs
He comes when you call him
How I am glad I own one.

David McBride (13)
Regent House School

MEMORY

Every morning at six,
Down the mine I go
There are all my friends,
With pain and sorrow on show.

Pushing crates, pulling loads,
Watching the sick people die.
I'm very tired, but cannot stop,
I have no time to cry.

My legs are tired,
But the whip still cracks,
His arm goes up and then,
The monster strikes our backs.

Although the pain can all be fixed,
When the day does end.
The sad thing is whatever you do,
The memories you can't mend.

Lorraine McKendrick (13)
Regent House School

SUNRISE ON A HILLSIDE

I sit alone on the hillside
With sleep still in my eyes,
I hear the birds begin to sing,
And the sun begins to rise.

The orange arms are reaching
Like fingers made of flames.
The fiery globe is shining
Like the torch of the Olympic Games.

He wanders the sky like a nomad
Searching for a place to dwell.
But always searching, never stops,
And will he, who can tell?

The sun is now much higher
As he waltzes across the sky,
A brandnew day is dawning,
And it meets only my eye.

Lynda McKnight (13)
Regent House School

SCHOOLDAYS

Monday comes again
And it's such a bore
'Cause I get school today
And the weekend's no more.

When Tuesday comes
There are only four days more
But I do have to work hard
And that'll mean my wrist might get sore.

Wednesday and Thursday are not all that bad
For PE and games keep me from going mad
I can run around and kick a football
I just hope I don't injure myself
If or when I happen to fall.

Friday seems to come around quite fast
I'll be able to put the school week in the past
I use my weekend to take a rest
From all the school work and the unit tests.

Sometimes I like school
But sometimes I don't
I guess it all really depends
And it all really comes down to
That I get to hang around with my friends.

Alain Elliott (13)
Regent House School

TO LUCY THE CAT

Beautiful, smooth, colourful fur,
A demanding miaow and a beautiful purr,
Her tail held up high with very great pride,
And whiskers long, but not very wide.

From her big friendly eyes to her smooth, slender paws,
She is a beauty to behold for me and for all,
A bubbly personality and a big jolly heart,
Her only let down is her big smelly fart!

Robin Griffith (12)
Regent House School

THE MILLENNIUM

Midnight is approaching,
Just 10 seconds to go
Now 5, 4, 3, 2 -
Darkness consumes the world.
Instead of cheering
There is screaming.

Will my whole future be
Shattered on this night?
Does so much of our world
Revolve around computers
That we will have nothing
Left when the clock strikes 12?
Will we start from the beginning
And rebuild our world?

There are so many questions
And no answers because
Nobody knows what fate
Has set for us. I just hope
That I never have to say
Hello to the Millennium Bug!

Rachel Ormsby (13)
Regent House School

SCHOOL

Oh no I'm late!
I should have woke at eight,
My bus will have gone by now,
My teacher and I will have a big row.

I didn't do my homework last night,
I was too busy flying my kite,
I really would hate another stupid detention,
But oh well, I guess there's no way of prevention.

So I got up and got on the 9.30am bus,
And as I had predicted my teacher created a huge fuss,
I was put in detention after school,
When I got home I realised I was a fool.

I don't see why we have to spend our time in a smelly old school,
But hey, I put up with it and that is very, very cool!

Selene Coey (12)
Regent House School

GRANNIES

Why is it grannies pull your cheeks,
Tell you you're beautiful,
And haven't seen you in weeks.
They coo and they smile,
And can't think of your name,
Is it Carol or Pam or something the same?

They come out with silly remarks,
On how you look like your dad.
When they say that,
I really get mad.

I know it's rather cruel,
For me to think this way,
But tell them just to save their jokes,
For some other day.

I know that from my words,
You really couldn't tell,
That I have a dear old granny,
Whom we call Granny Bell.

Sara Lindores (13)
Regent House School

MEALS

My mum always says that the best way to start the day,
is with a healthy, nutritious breakfast.
What should I have? It's such a hard choice,
should I have fruit, toast or cereal,
or just my usual fry up?

Lunch is always in the canteen.
We all queue up and we are eventually served,
by that time we are all really hungry.
I normally choose the unhealthy food,
chips, sausages and a cold can of coke.

How I can't wait until dinner time,
after a hard day at school,
to see what Mum has prepared for me.
Will it be chicken or even beef?
Oh no! It's peas and carrots.

Peter Thompson (13)
Regent House School

DARKNESS

The dark is what
I fear most,
Its endless blackness,
As you lie and stare.
All around you it lingers,
It won't go away until it is light,
And then it disappears,
Like a puff of smoke on a windy day.

But don't think once that it is gone,
Because it's only hiding,
And soon it will come back again,
Just when the sun begins to set,
It will come, it will come.

It will creep along the ground,
And up through the trees,
And no one person, animal or thing can escape it.
It covers the earth like a web,
You can't break free until it disappears,
You're trapped, until dawn.

Danielle Harper (13)
Regent House School

MY BEDROOM

My bedroom is my special room
I think of it as a haven
I stay it in until my stomach
Tells me it is cravin'
So downstairs I go to raid the fridge
And back upstairs with more supplies
With my TV book beneath my arm
And lots of crisps and apple pies.

My PlayStation is my best friend
I play with it from dawn till dusk
Until my mother says I must
Come downstairs to eat my tea
Then do my homework, my ABCs
Then it is time to lay my head
Upon my pillow, on my bed.

Ryan Cherry (12)
Regent House School

HALLOWE'EN

It's late October and it's cold and wet
And trick or treaters are coming I bet
There'll be angels and ghosts and all the rest
And all the kids are fighting over who looks the best

There'll be knocking at your door
And you'll get a terrible bore
When they say that stupid rhyme
They say it nearly every time

So you give them money and maybe a sweet
Because they're dressed up from head to feet
Some look great and some look bad
And some just look really sad

So now it's over and the costumes go away
To come back out another day
So now it's over, no more song or rhyme
But the next thing coming is Christmas.

Simon White (13)
Regent House School

ETHEL'S HOUSE

We knew we weren't supposed to
But we wanted to go in.
Its walls with faded blood
And its hist'ry doused with sin.

There were seven in the family
But the parents went insane
And somewhere in the garden
Lie five children's remains.

It seems that John (the father)
Had had too much to drink
And with a hook and rusty chain
Killed the kids (or so we think).

And after he had slain them all
A gory, frightful sight
He buried them in shallow graves
On that rainy, fearful night.

When Ethel found the children
And all of them were dead
She got a sharpish wood-axe
And lobbed off Johnny's head.

Not buried with the children
But thrown into a stream
And Ethel looking down at him
Gave out a mournful scream.

Now Hallowe'en is coming soon
With firework-filled skies
And we all wait with baited breath
To see if the dead will rise . . .

Ryan Jendoubi (12)
Regent House School

MY SANCTUARY

Daylight begins to fade and go
The lights all soon go on
The curtains are all drawn
The day is nearly gone.

I really enjoy this time
I think of it as mine
I'm able to wind down
And eventually go to bed.

My bed is my sanctuary
It's so warm, safe and secure
The cares and worries of the day
All soon become no more.

I pull the covers up to my chin
And rest my weary bones
The heat soon envelops me
And soon I drift away.

I sometimes hear the wind and rain
Lashing on the window pane
Occasionally I spare a thought
For a travelling man.

But usually I'm safe and comfortable
I'm happy in my bed each night
I'm so cosy and warm.

My happiness soon fades away
By the dawning of the morn
But I know it's only hours away
Before I return to my sanctuary.

Jonathan Morrow (12)
Regent House School

WHAT IS A POEM?

A poem can be a number of things,
A group of letters, words or lines.
It can be very short or very long,
But doesn't have to rhyme.

You can make it up as you go along,
Take excess amount of time.
But still it is a group of words,
Which do not have to rhyme.

A poem, let me think of one,
I'm doing it right now,
If it's good or if it's bad.

It normally has a steady beat,
But you have to keep in time.
When you are reading through my poem,
It's up to you what way it rhymes.

Neil Dougan (14)
Regent House School

THE EAGLE

Far away in lonely lands
Where the sea beneath the mountain crawls,
Where the sun beats down, an eagle stands,
Scanning from his mountain walls.

He searches with his fiery eyes,
For prey above and beneath the sea.
With outspread wings he soars the skies,
Then sits majestic, so wild and free.

Lindsey Blair (13)
Regent House School

My Little Friend

My little friend,
The one that no one can see,
Is actually very good to me.
He'll bring me sweets and he'll bring me toys,
So many that I'll never bore any boys.

My little friend has dark black hair,
And skin that is very fair,
With his big brown eyes and his chubby cheeks,
And I must not forget his mouth that always speaks.

His favourite food is ice-cream and jelly,
So, that's why he has such a big belly!
But as I get older the time will come,
For me to no longer have an imaginary chum!

Kellie Jordan (12)
Regent House School

Golden Season

Growth slows down,
The garden takes a rest,
The colour changes before my eyes,
Blazing red flowers are replaced by golden leaves.

The trees are soon naked,
Their clothes lie upon the ground,
Their work is complete,
They cover the ground like a golden blanket.

Night calls earlier,
Evening lasts longer,
Autumn is here.

Katrina Russell (12)
Regent House School

THE CHRISTMAS TREE

The Christmas tree stands in the middle of the room,
shining in all its glory.
It stands tall and proud
with its lights flickering in the stillness.

It is decorated with balls, tinsel, ribbon and holly,
all to make it beautiful.
As days go by it is harder to see
with all the presents big and wee.

When it is all over,
we have to say goodbye.
But we shall do it again next year,
so goodbye Christmas tree.

Colin Dickson (12)
Regent House School

HALLOWE'EN

Hallowe'en is coming
And the shops are getting filled with goodies.
There're bangers going off and there
On TV, there are really good movies!

The pumpkin's getting lit
And the witches are about.
There are Hallowe'en rhymers running around
Can't you hear the banshees shout?

I just can't wait for the Hallowe'en parties
And all the things there are to do.
Hallowe'en rhyming, scaring people,
I like Hallowe'en, don't you?

Rachel McKeown (12)
Regent House School

THE HOLIDAY

Driving through the city
Noises are all you can hear
Car horns beeping, people shouting
All the hustle and bustle.

Finally away from the noise
Into the peaceful countryside
No beeping or people shouting -
Just silence.

Driving through the countryside
Birds singing, sun is shining
The peacefulness is brilliant
There is not one loud sound.

Walking along Lough Erne
Listening to the swish of the water
The bubbling of the stream
And feeling the light wind in your face.

Walking through the fields
Seeing that beautiful view
Watching the cows graze in the distance
And looking out beyond the horizon.

I think about going back to the city,
Back to all the noise
Peacefulness is gone, the silence broken
Never to be heard again!

Natasha Gilliland (13)
Regent House School

POOR OLD MO

Poor old Mo, she's gone away,
back to London, there to stay.
So now folks, let's wish her well,
as her peace agreement she found hard to sell.
Doctor Ian was the first to say she must go,
but it was not long before she had many a foe.
In Ulster she tried so hard friends to make,
but soon learned it was not a piece of cake.
She hosted a concert at the Waterfront Hall,
but to poor old Mo not one kind look did they befall.
To Portadown's Garvaghy Road one day she went,
to make peace between the two sides she was bent.
To Brendan McKenna she tried to talk,
till he kept saying, 'The orange men will not walk.'
She talked and talked with all her zeal,
but no agreement with McKenna could she seal.
Cross Portadown she went with all her will,
let us see if I can make a friend on Drumcree Hill.
'Twas here friendship she hoped to crown,
till Harold Gracey said, 'Garvaghy we must get down.'
Mo said 'I've tried and tried with all my might,
now once again I can find no agreement in sight.'
So dear old Mo, you've tried so hard,
let's hope some day you will find your just reward.
So dear old Mo, I say farewell to thee,
maybe someday you will return for all to see.

Keith Currie (12)
Regent House School

LEAVES

One day
I stared out,
As I sat there
They fell,
Never stopping
On and on.

With branches bare and
Ground brown with leaves.
Others stay there,
Green
So high,
Why
Oh why?

Sonya Ritchie (13)
Regent House School

THE MOUNTAIN

The mountain rises out of the mist,
Like a giant of purple heather.
Surrounded by a million greenflies
Which look like a coat of green velvet.

As I ascended this beast of a hill,
I thought pensively of
What this mountain has seen,
What we have done to its countryside.

And then I recalled how we
Had wrecked this gentle giant,
His country and family by
Building on its slope and fields.

Paul Grant (13)
Regent House School

CATS

These creatures are so amazing,
So amazing they are to me,
They walk about with their heads held high,
So proud they seem to be.
They roam the streets every night,
With their eyes lit up by the moonlight,
And every time they see a mouse,
They always stand poised ready to pounce.

These creatures are so puzzling,
So puzzling they are to me,
One minute they want affection,
And the next they want let be.
Sometimes they want sleep,
And other times they want to play,
I guess we'll never understand,
But just play along anyway!

Jenny Donaghey (13)
Regent House School

STARS IN SIGHT

I look to the sky at night
Especially when the stars are in sight.
They always twinkle, they're always bright
Some say it's gas burning throughout the night
But I think they are angels' lookout lights
Most of them glide without sight
They never worry, they never fight
When I'm down and feeling blue
Seeing that perfect sight
Cheers me up all that night.

Allan Stewart (13)
Regent House School

SCHOOL

I go to school, I wonder why,
I have to go to school?
To learn, they say, to get ahead,
What's wrong with lying in my bed?

I go to school, I wonder why,
I have to go to school?
In HE to make buns for tea,
But surely my mum does that for me!
In maths to learn how to count
But I never have the right amount.
Unless it comes to time for sport,
When last two periods I abort.
I take the field, I play the game,
Back to lessons tomorrow, what a *shame!*

Stephen Marshall (12)
Regent House School

A POEM FOR HALLOWE'EN

Come taste this witch's stew,
Made from her own special brew.
She could pick on you,
But be careful - this stew could kill you!
Made from monster guts,
Cats' eyes, dogs' tails
And of course her own special potion,
Which is too disgusting to describe.
If I were you I'd keep away,
From this wicked, dirty, wise old witch.
She can make you twitch.

Grant Dugan (13)
Regent House School

GETTING TO SLEEP

It was 11 o'clock on a cold Sunday night,
I lay in bed listening for sounds outside.
I thought about the events that happened that day,
And how it had sailed past.
It was a terrible, stormy night,
The rain could be heard belting against the window,
The wind could be heard whistling through the cracks in the walls.
My eyelids were as heavy as lead,
As red as fire.
I wanted to sleep.
All of a sudden there was a crash,
I decided to investigate.
I tiptoed to my window,
And pushed the blinds back cautiously.
There was a skinny figure running wildly down the street,
It was a cat!
Disappointed that it was nothing else,
I staggered to my bed.
I looked to my clock,
It read 12.42am.
I was so tired and I closed my eyes.
I felt so exhausted the next day.
My clock, 8.20am.
I forgot to set my alarm.
I was half an hour late!

Darren Wong (13)
Regent House School

THE WAR

The war!
The blood!
The pain!
I think that
we are all insane!

Why try to make
stronger guns,
when we should
try to save
our future sons?

Why do we go to war again?
Is it to ensure that
blood can cause
another stain?

Soon we will destroy our lands,
but now, think about the clans
who spilt their blood,
to save this barren waste.

But soon we'll say
'Let's all go to war again
and see the blood trickle,
then stain the white cloths
of peace.'

Richard Lyttle (13)
Regent House School

SCHOOLDAYS

I wake up in the hazy light,
And start to play out my day.
I'll have some fun,
Play some golf.
At least I don't have to go,
And waste my time in school.
Oh no!
My mum's brought breakfast on a tray,
It must be a school day.

So I get up,
Put on my clothes,
And get washed.
I eat breakfast,
And pack my bag with all those books,
Will this day ever end?
It seems like it's been hours already.

I board the car,
And wave goodbye,
To the day I never had.
Oh why do I have to spend
Another day in prison.
I arrive, but what?
There's no one here.
The place is totally deserted.
I look at my watch,
I knew it was a Saturday!

William McAllister (14)
Regent House School

SIX ROAD ENDS

Where the country meets the town,
In the midst of County Down,
It's the meeting of the ways,
Like the sun's radiating rays.

The sheep are quite unaware,
Of the heavy traffic passing there,
Tractors are in no hurry,
Unlike the townsfolk - in a scurry.

The stench of cows' manure,
Is a smell that some can't endure,
But to the people of the land,
It makes them just feel grand!

To be free of all the city smoke,
To be healthy, fit and outdoor folk,
With the green fields all around,
Quite like a rolling eiderdown.

The tranquillity which is shattered,
A screech and glass is scattered,
Will the people of the town,
Not learn to *slow right down?*

The cows don't run about,
The birds have time to sing,
People don't have to shout,
It's an extraordinary thing!

I hope we'll long be friends,
I and the *six road ends.*

Kyle Curran (13)
Regent House School

SNAKES

S is for the skin that they shed off every year.
N is for the noise the rattle makes.
A is for Anaconda that hunts and kills its prey.
K is for the kitty cats that it eats.
E is for elastic bodies that help them move around.
S is for the sound it makes when it hisses.

Andrew Ward (12)
Regent House School

FLOWERS

Flowers are beautiful things,
they start off as a seed
as tiny as a crumb
but there are many in a packet,
making sure there is a blossom in one.

And when they blossom in their splendour
brings the beautiful smell of summer.

The bees are busy, buzzing around,
the nectar waiting to be found.

The nice smells, the long nights,
the bright flowers,
ending.

Summer is growing shorter,
the bees are hiding in their nest,
the flowers are drooping down to the ground,
they go so low, they cannot be found.

Charlene Conway (11)
St Colman's High School, Ballynahinch

THE GREEN MAN IN THE GARDEN

Green man in the garden
Staring from the tree,
Why do you look so long and hard
Through the pane at me?

Your eyes are dark as holly,
Of sycamore your horns,
Your bones are made of elder branch,
Your teeth are made of thorns.

His hair is made of grass,
His skin is a brighter green,
There he stands among the leaves,
Quite plain to be seen.

His spaceship is at my front door,
I can see the beaming light,
I often wondered what it was,
Shining so bright at night.

So if you ever see this man,
Do not be afraid,
He only wants to be your friend,
So please come to his aid.

Eamon Kelly (11)
St Colman's High School, Ballynahinch

A Frightening Experience

Once there was an eerie old castle on top of a mountain hill
There it stood so silent and still, unseen and unheard during day
But when night fell, spooky sounds and screams could be heard for
miles and miles around, but during the day not a sound.

I explored the castle one night to see what was going on
I walked up the path and there it stood, so spooky and so still
As I walked through the door, a song could be heard, gradually it
stopped, the door shut behind me as I stood there in shock.

Walking up the stairs, creek, creek, creeks
As the town down below sleeps, sleeps, sleeps.
I hear voices whisper in the room beside me
I look inside, nobody to be seen.
Suddenly down the bottom of the long landing a person of a ghost
could be seen just standing
It suddenly ran for me, it just went through me.

I run down the stairs, as they fall behind me
I hear the ghost call 'Get out, understand me'
Down the path, back to my house
I tell my mum the castle is definitely haunted
Of course she doesn't believe me as she taunted there's no such
thing as ghosts.

Every night I think of my adventure
But still the castle stands so spooky and so still
On top of the mountain hill.

Megan Short (11)
St Colman's High School, Ballynahinch

MY SECRET PLACE

Beyond a high wall, up at Nan's
Lies a stretch of brightly coloured land
A carpet of beauty for all to see
But the one who cares for it most is me.
I call it my beautiful summer place,
My garden of beauty, my land of grace
Where rosebuds bloom a royal red
And bright-eyed birds come to be fed;
Where the sun at dawn colours the trees
And from the south creeps a whispering breeze
While I am there, the world's at peace
There is no fighting, there is no grief
This is where I like to be
Away from harsh reality.

Kelly Doyle (11)
St Columban's College, Kilkeel

MY SECRET PLACE

It has a hidden loveliness
That only I can see
Trees are clothed in green leaves
Hanging moist and free.
A stream makes quiet murmuring sounds
Birds sing songs of praise
The sky is shrouded in flimsy cloud
The sun's a golden haze.
It's there in flowers and weeds grow tall
In this world of loveliness
I am lord of all.

Sally-Anne Hennity (16)
St Columban's College, Kilkeel

WONDERING WHY
(A response to a family tragedy)

Lost, lonely, devastated . . .
I wonder
My fault . . .
All my fault?
Stop!

Everything happening, life sparkling -
Stopped.

Did I do anything wrong?
Failed to see?
Failed to hear?
Failed to love?
Never!

Deserved to live?
Why me?
Why did they die?
Why me?
Always to bear the guilt?

Searing tears falling,
People staring blankly in shock,
Murmured regrets,
Wondering why.

Is this just a nightmare?
Am I going to wake up?
Lost, lonely, devastated . . .
Unbearable.

Everything they did I loved
Everything I did they cherished.
Inseparable in life,
Now sundered apart.

Left without them,
Wondering why.

Tanya Morgan (16)
St Columban's College, Kilkeel

MY SECRET PLACE

In my secret place I am free
To look at beauty.
There is no fee
To watch the sun
Like a golden kite
Rising on its victory flight;
To watch the clouds
Of fluffy wool
Float giddy and careless
Like happy fools;
To watch the larks circle high
Swooping and singing
As they fly.
In my secret place
There is no fee
To look at beauty
Or to be free.

Siobhan O'Hare (15)
St Columban's College, Kilkeel

THE STARS IN THE SKY

Joined together by love . . .
By love?
Nothing can separate us . . .
Can love be everlasting?

Am I in love?
Can I take that chance?
How can I be sure?
I change . . .
Love can change.
Do the stars change?
I am in love.

It changed.

He has gone.
Time spent with him . . .
So much time,
I knew him so well.
He would have given me the stars in the sky.

Now he can't.

What shall I do,
Can I still go on?

Nobody can understand,
Words drown me,
Yet I can't talk to anyone.
The words seem so meaningless.

The stars in the sky . . .
If I look,
Will I see?
Will you see me?

Joined together by love,
My love is everlasting.

Rosemary Trainor (15)
St Columban's College, Kilkeel

GUY THE GORILLA

I wish this tragic dream would end,
So I can go and play with my friends,
I'm sick and tired of this stupid zoo,
I don't like being here and neither would you.

I used to live in a lovely place,
With trees and vines and a soft covered base,
I liked it there, I liked it a lot.
It was better than here,
It was sunny and hot.

Then one day two men came to my house,
They put me in a cage and I was as quiet as a mouse,
My cage rattled as we went along,
That was my last time I saw my friends because I had gone.

I ended up in this alienated world,
My mind was muddled up,
It swirled and it swirled,
I want to go home, back to the heat,
So I'm not cramped up oh so nice and neat.

Nicola Madden (13)
St Columban's College, Kilkeel

LONELINESS

An old woman
Living just around the corner,
Her name is Mary.

Sometimes I visit her.
'She's such a kind old lady'
And mother says
'She is so good with animals.'

Good with animals,
So lonely,
No one to talk to.

An old lady
Waving out through her window,
Her name is Mary.

Sometimes I visit her.
'I visit my friend,'
Mary says
'Out in the country.'

Out in the country?
I smile and listen.
There are no friends,
There is no country.

She dreams . . .
She hopes . . .
Sometimes I visit her.

The clock on the wall -
Always slow,
Becoming slower.

An old lady
Looking through faded photographs,
Her name is Mary.

Sometimes I visit her.
'Do you want me to do anything
For you Mary?'
I ask,
She smiles.

Catherine McKay (15)
St Columban's College, Kilkeel

AUTUMN

Autumn is coming,
While summer is leaving,
The blackberries are juicy,
The brambles are sharp!

The leaves are all falling,
Off the beautiful trees.

Everyone's harvesting their
Crops at dawn,
The mice, and the rats
Are trying to hide.

The days get shorter,
While the nights get longer,
The whole place is dark
At half past eight.

Catherine Carr (14)
St Columban's College, Kilkeel

THE BIG SECRET

I went to that place,
I was told not to go.
But being me I did,
I just had to find out.

A door creaked open,
A cat ran past.
A light bulb fell,
A window banged closed.
I looked down,
There it was,
I now know the secret,
That shouldn't have come out,
I now know I shouldn't have gone.

Edel Magee (15)
St Columban's College, Kilkeel

STORM

When the wind is strong
And the tide is high
I lie and listen
As time goes by
On the shore or in my boat
When the sea's like this
I'm full of hope
The high waves crash
Along the sandy beach
The strong wind howls
And the seagulls screech
When the great white gannet start to swoop and dive
Then deep inside I feel alive.

James Clarke (16)
St Columban's College, Kilkeel

DENYING

(A response to J Steinbeck's 'Of Mice And Men' reflecting
on the experiences of Curley's wife, a lonely, neglected wife
who dies in sad circumstances.)

Sad, lonely . . . trapped.
Trapped?
By what?
A force?
A bond?
An unbearable bond.

Marriage?
My husband denying me,
Me.

'Curley's wife.'
Have I no name?
I think, I talk . . . I dreamed.

The men sneer.
He is watching me,
Controlling,
Denying.
Alone on a ranch,
Sun-baked, life-sapping.
I'm trapped.

Love?
I dreamed of Curley by my side.
A bond
An unbreakable bond
Together on a ranch,
Sun-fired, life generating.

Denied communion,
I die.

Jennifer Archer (16)
St Columban's College, Kilkeel

BLACKBERRIES

Along the lane
as far as the eye can see
are briars with ripened blackberries
waiting for me.

With the biggest tin I could find
off I set
to pick lots of berries
at my granny's request.

She prepares jam and jellies
all made from blackberries sweet.
Picking carefully one by one
minding the thorns
I fill my tin so full.

Return home with the sun on my back
feeling proud and contented
my tin is jam-packed.

Buzzing, whizzing
bees swarm around my tin
I run to escape
knowing I can't win.

Tossing, tumbling a few at a time
I finally reach home
with a few on the bottom.
I feel it wasn't worthwhile
but open the door
and Granny gives me a smile,
'Don't worry, son,
I have a tin with a lid
for you tomorrow!'

Conor McComb (13)
St Columban's College, Kilkeel

SCARED

It's a noise.
There's something there . . .
In that room,
Its shadow swallowing the doorway,
The floorboards creaked.
What was that noise?
I don't know, do I?
I crept towards the doorway
And slowly opened it.
Was there anybody there?
No.
Perhaps it's gone away then,
But then I heard something,
I froze in terror.
The floorboards creaked,
Something was coming up the stairs.
It might be a g-g-g-h-ost - nah
I don't think I know what it is.
'Who's there?' I shouted.
Silence
Then I heard voices
'You're scared,' one voice said
'No I'm not'
'Yes you are'
'So are you then.'
The voices stopped.
The door slammed shut.
Dare I go out?
Just when you think it's safe,
That you imagined it . . .
You feel its warm breath on your neck!

Steven Curran (13)
St Columban's College, Kilkeel

SEPARATED

Gypsies!
Itinerants!
Travellers.

Angry voices,
Strongly expressed views,
Public opinion,
Shattered lives.

Separated by
Hatred,
Prejudice,
Fear of facing our conscience.

No facilities
No permanence
No integration
No understanding

Separated by
Indifference.
Apathy,
Cruelty of words we leave unsaid.

Gypsies?
Itinerants?
Fellow travellers -

Questioning our humanity.

Ian Rooney (15)
St Columban's College, Kilkeel

LONELINESS

Loneliness -
A darkness within me.
Every day the same,
Nothing to do,
Nowhere to go,
And no one to talk to.

Dark, rainy days,
Darkness engulfing.
Trapped in a space of my own,
Lost without direction.

No laughter,
No warmth,
No togetherness.
Waiting -
Hoping . . .
But the darkness deepens.

Friendship -
Someone to talk to,
To trust,
To share the light.

Emmett Sloan (16)
St Columban's College, Kilkeel

LOVE... WHAT DOES IT MEAN?

I never knew there was so much love . . .
Two people brought together by an empyrean bond.

Entwined in each other
Like vines gracefully growing,
Growing and nourishing each other
Each and every day.

Growing close or further apart?
Love should come from deep down in the heart
Deeply felt but no scars leaving.
Joys will be shared, tears will be shouldered
So the love will grow
And not be torn apart.

Chocolates and roses can bring delight
Sparks can fly and electricity charge -
Indeed images abound . . .
But love is oh so real -
Heart-warming and
Life giving.

Arlene McDowell (16)
St Columban's College, Kilkeel

AT NINE O'CLOCK

At nine o'clock in the morning
My daughter said to me:

'The sun and the sky are gracious.
The dawn and the dusk
Hold an excellence and beauty.
Grass radiates greener every day.
Mountains grow taller
As the hours go by.
Crystal blue waters
Rage madly towards beach stones.
The world is wonderful!
Dizzy with brightness!
So, why are you so grey,
Daddy?
Why do you look so sad?'

Catrina Anderson (15)
St Columban's College, Kilkeel

FIRST DAY OF SCHOOL

Big boys bang and bounce,
Lots of lads in the library,
Students study straightforward work,
Teachers tell boys tales,
Francis fries food in the kitchen,
Harry's hanging high from the trees,
The teachers are running around like bees,
That's the *first day of school.*

Philip Mills (11)
St Patrick's Grammar School, Downpatrick

TO MY GRANDFATHER

I remember all the things you did for me,
All the things you gave me,
This is because you were dear to me,
Because you were everything to me.

I remember your voice,
Asking if I was alright,
And your touch,
Picking me up when I was down.

At the end of the day,
You were best,
And you will always be with me.

Ryan Savage
St Patrick's Grammar School, Downpatrick

MY GRANDA

My granda was fairly small,
He walked about in no great rush,
Pretending to be so tall,
With his loyal old dog, Bush.

He sat on his worn-down chair,
Clicking his false teeth with his tongue,
Puffing smoke from his pipe into the air,
And saying one time 'If only I were young.'

My granda wasn't lonely and sad,
He was good fun,
He did with what he had,
I'm glad I was his grandson.

Conor Smyth (14)
St Patrick's Grammar School, Downpatrick

I HATE FOOTBALL

I hate football
It's really true
It drives me up the wall,
To see people play and do.
The advertisements they put on:
Eat football
Sleep football
Drink football
Well I've put on something
to advertise and surprise:
Hate football!
Stop football!
Stop, stop, stop football!
So there you go my point's been sighted
So get off my TV screen you Man United!

Christopher Campbell (11)
St Patrick's Grammar School, Downpatrick

CHANGING ROOMS

Students come and change,
Bears getting ready for battle,
Bears charge for the food,
Students galloping for the ball,
After a long battle,
The bears rinse in the tropical waterfalls,
And the foam lies on the river top.
A whirlpool takes all the water and foam,
And the waterfalls stop.
Bears change and get ready for another battle,
A battle in the classrooms.

Alan McAlinden (12)
St Patrick's Grammar School, Downpatrick

THE NIGHT BEFORE SCHOOL

As I looked out the window at the night sky,
In my stomach there was more than one butterfly.
For I was thinking of the day ahead,
And meeting new teachers which I thought I would dread.

At least I didn't have to get the bus,
So there wouldn't be as much fuss.
The school was big, that I knew,
And my friends that where going, would be few.

Would I get lost or find my way?
I knew I would find out the very next day.
So as I lay down and tried to sleep
I thought of the rules I'd have to keep.

James Morrison (11)
St Patrick's Grammar School, Downpatrick

MY ROOM

My room is a jungle,
My friends are explorers.

My bed is mountains high and low,
The clothes like trees covering the ground.

The shoes are hills high and low,
The light is the sun that towers down.

A toucan bird flies by,
Some tigers are in through the trees.

The heat is like a tropical breeze,
The buildings are rolled-up socks.

Steven McMullan (11)
St Patrick's Grammar School, Downpatrick

FAMINE TIMES

A cold wind blew,
And the mist was strong,
How long will this hunger go on and on?

I looked in their faces,
And into their eyes.
The horror that struck me,
Took me by surprise.

I smelt that room,
So musty and raw.
The stench of death,
Travels on and on.

I walked the road,
Much travelled upon,
To the Promised Land,
I travel on and on.

Ryan Rogan (13)
St Patrick's Grammar School, Downpatrick

FEARS

The night before school I was sitting in bed
Thinking of the hard work and books to be read.
Worried about teachers and thinking about getting lost,
Afraid of getting kicked, punched and tossed.

When going to school, sitting in the car
I was wondering, would I last for even an hour?
I was worried about missing the bus
And when I get home, my mum making a fuss.

David Clarke (11)
St Patrick's Grammar School, Downpatrick

ODE TO A LOVED ONE

Back then when we were free
You and I had nothing
.And nothing mattered to me.

Our lives meant nothing,
Yet, they've always meant so much,
Each day was everything.

Each carefree day,
And every passing minute,
You went further away.

And when it came,
Our time grew short
You lay there . . . lame.

From that day on,
I've thought of you,
From that day on,
Our love was true.

Ryan Walsh (14)
St Patrick's Grammar School, Downpatrick

THE BUS

Boys barging and ganging and beating on the bus,
It's all such a fuss.
Girls who run to the bus and boys who walk to the bus,
Galloping and guzzling like animals free from the zoo.
The bus brings everybody, bustling, bothering, banging
and bouncing.
There is a lot of action.
On the bus is a lot of fun.

Mark Bell (12)
St Patrick's Grammar School, Downpatrick

GRANNY

Granny you were quiet,
You never said a word,
You were like an angel,
Sitting on a stool.

You were giving to the poor,
Then I knew you were pure.
You never said a thing if you could say nothing good,
You just said hello because you knew you should.

You lived for your family - granny,
Yes I see it's true,
When you ate you ate for us,
But when you couldn't eat, you breathed for us.

But when you were in hospital your lungs collapsed.
You could not breathe,
All that was left was your heart of love,
It may have stopped, but the loving will not.

Gerard Savage (13)
St Patrick's Grammar School, Downpatrick

CHARLES

C heeky boys shout and scream.
H assling boys annoying the teachers.
A fraid to teach him all the teachers.
R ows he starts and ends.
L azy he is every day.
E nticing children to curse and swear.
S taying behind after school.

James Davey (11)
St Patrick's Grammar School, Downpatrick

MY GRANNY

My granny, fit as a fiddle, having brilliant holidays all over the
world with her children.
Money or presents every time we visited, all she could do was give.
But now she isn't with us, we can only bring back memories.

We now fill a house, empty of her but her presence can still be felt.
Her children all around us bringing back her life.
A constant rumble filled the air, stories of old times bring happy
memories of her.

Smoke filled the air making it musty and sour and the sick feeling
reminded us of death.
Each family member hurt, with an unhappy smile on their faces trying
to keep our hopes up, but not succeeding as they couldn't cure
her death.
But in the end, we must move on and if she saw us today,
She would be happy at our recovery, from the time she passed away.

Matthew Quinn (14)
St Patrick's Grammar School, Downpatrick

THE NIGHT BEFORE SCHOOL

The night before school
I lost my cool and went completely mad.
I couldn't sleep so I counted sheep and got lost after 54.
I rolled about wondering what the school would be like:
The teachers giving you loads of homework
And making you do loads of class work.
I thought I would get lost
In this big school
And not remember a single rule.

Christopher Malone (12)
St Patrick's Grammar School, Downpatrick

COME BACK SOON

I remember how you went
On that windy winter day.
I saw the tears pour out of your eyes,
I knew you didn't want to go.

I took a great smell of the country air
To help me cope with this loss.
But now any time I smell the air
All I can think of is you.

I can remember the good times we had
When we played football in the park.
I can also remember the bad times
But think I shouldn't.

Goodbye,
Please, come back soon!

Liam Rogan (13)
St Patrick's Grammar School, Downpatrick

IN THE JUNGLE

My bedroom is a jungle,
I sleep in the bushes which is my bed.
I climb up the trees, my ladder is the tree.
The lion pounces at me, my sister long and tall.
She pounces at the parrot and kills it, no more chirping.
The TV is now off, what is there to do?
The keyboard begins to sing, it is a bird in the tree.
The rain made the jungle dark, the curtain pulled across.
I hear my mother shouting, like a toucan chirping.
That means it's time for tea.

Gareth McGreevy (11)
St Patrick's Grammar School, Downpatrick

MY MEMORY

I was in my house playing the computer,
In the distance I could hear screams and sirens,
What could it be?
I looked up at my friend's house,
And I said, who could it be?

A rush of airiness came all over me,
So I ran up to see what I could see,
I asked the mum, who could it be?
She told me the story and that I could not believe,
A lot of sadness came over me that day.

I could smell the oil from the garage,
I dared not look into see him there,
I was thinking what had come over him,
The paramedics were hard at work,
Nothing could be done to save him know.

The next night I saw him in his bed
All quiet, all white, so still,
I still could not believe,
The whole house was quiet
And to this day I still don't know why.

Can you tell me why?
That is all I want to know
He always told me jokes,
I miss him very much.

Conor Trainor (14)
St Patrick's Grammar School, Downpatrick

DEAR GRANNY

You never got your telegram from the Queen
I really had some great times
Playing cards (poker)
I haven't told Mum yet.

Me fetching your cosy slippers
Giving you tablets,
The salt and water,
Your old stories, the Titanic and when you were a child.

I will never forget the smell
Honeyrose and peppermint, when you entered the room.
The smell in the living room,
Burning coal from the fire.

You were really sweet, kind and generous
During your time on Earth.
Always under doctor's care
Me and Mum coming to visit
Every Thursday night.

I miss your stories and playing cards
But that's not all,

Granny I miss you loads.

Rest in Peace.

John Rooney (13)
St Patrick's Grammar School, Downpatrick

CRAZY DAY

Herds of animals stampeding around
Bumper cars in the playground.
Sergeant Majors bawling commands
Coming from where the teachers stand.

Indians scalping if the hair is too long
As they sing their battlecry song.
Sardine cans which take us home
Bully boys frothing foam.

People laugh as they stare
At the uniform we wear.
I'm going into a new class
Oh no, the summer's gone too fast!

Damian Ritchie (11)
St Patrick's Grammar School, Downpatrick

SCHOOL

The teachers are fierce dogs barking.
Bugging you are books and pens
Putting you to sleep.

In the classroom teachers are gorillas
Going crazy at you because you haven't
Done your homework.

Tables are rocks, hard and uncomfortable.
When you hit yourself on them you cry.

Edwin McKibben (11)
St Patrick's Grammar School, Downpatrick

ONE MAN AND HIS GUITAR

I could never see what you wanted,
Your ideas were not words but notes,
Musical notes that spoke,
And they spoke when you played the guitar.

When I was distraught,
Your notes could play thought,
Your notes could strum laughter,
In a greyness of mind.

You played your guitar and ignored other's thoughts,
Your spirit soared away with the notes,
And in that sea of meaningful sound,
Still my brother floats.

Adam Wilson (13)
St Patrick's Grammar School, Downpatrick

BEDROOM JUNGLE

My room is a jungle.
The mess and rubbish are trees,
There is no need for my bin
But I keep it anyway.

My bed is my lair
Like a lion I sleep.
It's cosy and comfy, ·
A tropical sun to keep me warm.

Brendan Scullion (11)
St Patrick's Grammar School, Downpatrick

BEDROOM

This room is a jungle full of papers.
It has a bouncy castle.
It is like a deserted village
With rotted old cars.

It has been destroyed by a giant.
The smell is horrid.
There is a cage,
The people inside are hard.

Oh no the giant is back
From his cave!
We are doomed!
We better hide.

Colman Trainor (11)
St Patrick's Grammar School, Downpatrick

MEMORY OF GRANNY

I can't sleep with all the worries,
My nan is dying in hospital.
The phone rang now I must hurry,
Like a motor car in full throttle.

I asked my dad, 'Is granny dead?'
The answer came with sorrow,
I went back to bed
It's a sad day tomorrow.

She's in heaven now with God,
But it's bad she had to suffer.
Tears were shed in the room,
But it's made us all tougher.

Christopher Sharvin (13)
St Patrick's Grammar School, Downpatrick

I Remember

I can remember you sitting there
Beside the warm golden fire,
With the dog on your lap and tea on the other.

I remember coming home from school,
You standing there cooking bread and pies.
You seeing me playing in the yard
And you coming out with the bucket in
your hand and asking for coal.

I remember your birthday when everyone was happy,
Everyone hugging you and giving you a kiss of good luck,
You sitting around the table
And people crowding around you like bees.

I remember your wake where everyone was sad
Lots of people came in and out shaking my dad's uncles',
and aunties' hands,
Offering sympathy for their troubles.

I remember you in your room
And everyone around you was crying,
Your cold body was a block of ice.
I was hoping you would dry out.

I remember in the chapel you lying at the front
And hundreds of people watching the priest pray over you.

I remember in the graveyard
You going into the ground.
I knew as soon as they lowered you
It would be the last I would see of you.

I really do miss you *granny.*

William Russell (13)
St Patrick's Grammar School, Downpatrick

VERONICA

Veronica was always on the go
Gardening and sun-bathing in the big garden.
With pruners and a wheel-barrow
Always in her hands.

Then one night she took bad
And was admitted into hospital
But she was independent
And asked for care at home.

Her house was sweet with flowers
And smelled of dog hairs
No more trips over to be greeted by a smile
Just a sad looking face.

There was never anything out of place
But now I bet she couldn't find anything
She also used to be plump
But now you can see her bones.

I'm glad she's in good care
because of her kindness and love
towards anything.

Christopher Tumelty (13)
St Patrick's Grammar School, Downpatrick

MY CLASSROOM

Teachers shout, lions roar,
Books piled up on my desk, the size of a giraffe,
Questions coming at every angle, a bird flies in the sky,
Students talking, a duck quacks.
My hand is writing quickly, like the ticking of a clock,
I am anxious for the bell to ring, an animal waits for his prey.

Shane McAnearney (12)
St Patrick's Grammar School, Downpatrick

THE BUS

The bus is a monster
That eats people at each stop.
And when they go to the next stop
It has digested and is ready for more.
When it stops, it makes a hiss and
That is it saying *ahhhhhh!*

David Gregge (11)
St Patrick's Grammar School, Downpatrick

HOME

Home is where the heart is,
Or so they say.
Home is where I feel safe and
Where I like to stay.
Home is warm and comfy,
Home is where I can be me,
Home is where I am loved,
And where I also feel free.

Eleanor Cassidy (11)
Sacred Heart Grammar School

TO LIVE . . .?

A dusty path less travelled,
The road to wealth and fame,
Travelled by the strong at heart,
Those who have become a household name.

Another lane well-worn,
Travelled often by the weak,
Those who travel only to work,
Day after day - week after week.

Which to use - is it really my choice,
Should I do what's right for them?
Or travel the one less travelled,
And find my wanted fame?

Follow in the footsteps
Of those who came before?
Or travel the one less travelled,
And face a family war?

To be or not to be,
In the words of one so great.
To live or not to live
The decision is too hard to make.

I know what my heart wants,
But my head keeps saying no.
To follow my head would destroy me,
Make my life so low.

A dusty path less travelled.
Another path well-worn.
I cannot decide which to travel,
My mind feels torn.

Denise McGuigan (14)
Sacred Heart Grammar School

WINTER

It's fast approaching, there's no escape,
Must stock up before it's too late.
The signs are there, the trees are bare,
Winter's coming, it's just not fair.

Short cold days, long dark nights,
Snow on the ground is a wonderful sight.
Children outside, there is a snowball fight,
Hats and scarves all wrapped up tight.

Despite the chill, it is the season of goodwill
And Christmas morning will bring many a thrill.
Turkey, ham, Christmas pudding and mince pies,
Is telling children of Santa Claus a lie?

New Year's Eve, December 31st,
The adults will quench their thirst,
With champagne, beer and whatever else,
No drink driving, let's hope they have the sense.

January, February is winter nearly spent,
Will they bring the beginning of lent?
Hope at last spring is nigh,
I hate winter - don't ask why.

Dervla Lynchehaun (12)
Sacred Heart Grammar School

MY LITTLE PAINTBOX

I have a little paintbox
With a rainbow on its lid.
I love to use the colours
Nestled in the tin.

White is the bride
Walking up the aisle.
The fleece upon the sheep
The snow upon the stile.

Red is the sun
Setting in the west.
Or a ladybird on a leaf
At rest.

Blue is the sky
On a summer's day.
Or a bluebell growing
Along the way.

Yellow is the daffodil
In the spring.
Or a yellow jewel
On a golden ring.

Brown are the leaves
Catching the autumn breeze.
Or the soil before the
Winter's freeze.

Green is the grass
I walk upon.
Green is the apple
I bite on.

These are the colours found within
My little paintbox made of tin.

Siobhan McNulty (11)
Sacred Heart Grammar School

THE SEASONS

First comes winter which we say we hate,
But really it's not too bad.
It snows, it rains, there are hurricanes!
And if we get wet we go mad!

After that we all calm down,
As spring comes along.
Flowers start growing, the wind stops blowing.
And birds fly about singing songs.

Next is summer which everyone loves,
But only if the weather is good.
No school, the swimming pool and the beach.
And no need for a coat with a hood.

Along comes autumn, the leaves start to fall.
In colours of orange, red and brown.
School starts again, oh what a shame!
But really we don't feel too down.

Bronagh McNally (12)
Sacred Heart Grammar School

STANDING IN THE QUEUE

Saturday in the supermarket, I dart from aisle to aisle,
I'm in a frightful hurry, too stressed out to smile.
Others too wear furrowed faces, no time for 'Please' or 'Sorry,'
Frenzied fingers grab the groceries and toss them in the trolley.

Shopping list complete, I bolt towards the check-out.
Stubborn trolley stops, sticks its hard neck out,
Sinks its steel claws in a fat lady's shins,
Cheeky clock on the wall looks down and grins!

Standing in the queue, it's already too late.
TV programme is over, I'm resigned to my fate.
Then all of a sudden I'm thinking, I'm focused,
I'm seeing, I'm hearing the things seldom noticed.

A young lad slips past, grabbing chocolates galore,
Then melts 'mid the masses, he's done it before!
Yet to blow his cover, 'twould be mean and vile,
A multi-national or a poor, hungry child?

I watch an old man slowly count out his money,
His feeble fingers know no hurry.
I'm eleven years old he's about . . . eighty-three,
Strange how he's got more time than me!

A mother now soothes a shrieking wean.
A cool dude picks his nose again,
But very discreetly, he looks well bred,
With 'Irish Times' and sun-bronzed head.

Queue suddenly stops, people shuffle and sigh,
I'm perfectly calm, no hurry have I!
There's wisdom in waiting no textbook can teach,
Lessons to learn that seemed out of reach.

I'm leaving the present, delving deep in the past,
My mind is ablaze, the scenes are all cast.
The soup kitchen queues of the famine I recall
And the queue for Titanic, the most poignant of all.

The millions of Jews forced to join the queue
By Hitler's henchmen back in World War Two
And Maximillian Kolbe who stood bravely in line,
Begging, 'Please, don't take *his* life! Take *mine!*

I'm back in the present; it's Saturday afternoon,
The line is much shorter, I'll get there real soon.
Thank God for the queues in the supermarket store.
May the queues of our ancestors happen no more.

Jane Rooney (12)
Sacred Heart Grammar School

WINTER

The outside world is unstirred, all physical life locked in slumber,
The earth is laden with droplets of majestic snow that gently flutter
in the arms of the wind,
The once-exposed trees, now have buds of a different assortment -
buds of snow all shapes and sizes,
No ducks ruminate the pond,
The sole use for the place that I have cherished memories of those
lazy summer days I spent swimming -
is a skating rink, where the brave twirl and swirl.
Frostbitten children in hats and gloves frolic in the snow, building
snowmen but soon return home because of the inclement weather.
Spider's webs glisten inhabited with frost, water that once dripped
spontaneously now has formed a diaphanous crystal alignment.

> *Winter isn't it a magnificent time?*

Danielle Holsgrove (12)
Sacred Heart Grammar School

SOCKS

My little dog has little brown feet
We call him Socks which I think is sweet.
He barks when he thinks he's going for a walk,
He'd be my best friend if only he could talk.

He hates to get washed but he has to get clean,
And it's terrible because I have to get mean.
But when it's all over he loves the hairdryer,
I sometimes get scared, I'll set him on fire.

When I come home he's barking at the gate,
He jumps up and down, he just can't wait!
Then at dinnertime, he scrapes at the door,
He gets all the scraps and still begs for more.

He gets scared when there's lightning and thunder,
Is it the noise or the flash? I often wonder.
He pricks up his ears when he hears other dogs bark,
And he really enjoys his trips to the park.

My little dog has a little winter coat,
He's so cute, he's my little dote.
My little dog is so cuddly and sweet
He's the nicest wee dog you'll ever meet.

Ciara Connolly (14)
Sacred Heart Grammar School

MY WONDERLAND

I would love to go to wonderland,
My wonderland is heaven,
Somewhere where I would go and shake God's hand,
But not go yet, I will wait until I am 77.

But hopefully when it is my time to go,
I will not go through any pain,
It is a long time yet so,
At least I will meet God again.

Geraldine Trainor (12)
Sacred Heart Grammar School

FULL MOON OF HALLOWE'EN

F angs of the vampire
U gliness of the witch
L aughter and cunning of the children
L ifting the door knocker and trick or treat.

M ore sweets, more candy
O h look at the silver moon
O ver the hills and
N ear paradise.

O wls hooting in the night
F lying off to catch their prey.

H allowe'en, oh, Hallowe'en
A ll the children shout
L ots of treats
L ots of tricks
O n those who will not give
W itches, goblins, ghosts and vampires
E at the candy, munch, munch, munch
E veryone is having fun
N obody is sad.

Except the victims of the tricks.

Ann-Louise McCamley (11)
Sacred Heart Grammar School

A Day In The Life Of Me

It's morning once again
I have to go to school.
To put on my socks and shoes
I sit down on my stool.
I start to eat my breakfast
I have to eat it quick.
Mother says don't eat it too fast
In case I might be sick.

I go to get the bus
And try to get a seat.
The day hasn't started
And I already feel dead-beat.
It is my first year at this school
I sometimes get lost.
If I am late for class
The teacher gets quite cross.

When I get home from school
All my work isn't done.
I have to do my homework
I don't have much time for fun.
We can read a book
Or watch a programme on TV
Before we go to sleep we can listen to CDs.

Andrea Murtagh (12)
Sacred Heart Grammar School

My Bedroom At Night

When I go to bed at night,
Without a worry or even a fright,
The toys in my room come to life.
(This will never happen 'til midnight)

The room is dark the motion is still,
Until there is a very slight fill.
This is when the toys come around
And dance along on the ground!

Judy Black (11)
Sacred Heart Grammar School

THE FORBIDDEN FOREST

Rotating, ruffling, shuffling sounds
Coming from forbidden grounds,
The homes of animals big and small,
The homes of plants short and tall.

Though forbidden, not so meek,
In the forest everyone speaks
Until the grand old tree will say,
'Let us halt now, let us call it a day.'

But during the night the beauty does not stop,
The leaves will twirl down from the top,
A bed of glorious leaves will lie
Upon the floor, opposite the sky.

Then the intruder will walk and talk,
Stamping the leaves and pulling the stalks.
The nature of our forest is gone,
The damage is done, it's all so wrong.

But nevertheless the forest is our forest;
It's like a farmer's own harvest.
No intruders will take it away,
The forbidden forest is here to stay.

Judith McLogan (12)
Sacred Heart Grammar School

MY DREAM

Last night I had a dream,
I dreamt that I could fly!
I saw the trees below me as I glided through the air,
Then I landed near a castle, which was really a dragon's lair!
The dragon was a humble beast,
With eyes as black as coal,
He invited me to a garden feast,
With a guest who was a mole!
We had hair soup and pork and we had some chocolate cake,
But Mr Mole could not find his fork, so he had to use a rake!

After dinner we sailed away in a tangerine submarine,
To an island where the bears are pink and the elephants are green.
The clouds had faces and talked about the weather
And the bramble bushes laughed and joked about the heather.
There were many other dragons and multicoloured moles,
Which jumped about on pogo sticks and hopped down tiny holes.

Then all of a sudden, the sky grew dark and the clouds began to cry,
Me and Mr Mole jumped down a hole, with the dragon very close by.
The mole gave a yelp and the dragon shouted 'Help!'
The island started to shake,
Then I found myself awake,
Just to hear my mother say,
'Get up for School!'

Aoife McCoy (11)
Sacred Heart Grammar School

FRIENDSHIP

Friends are always there for you
They're with you no matter what you do.
No matter what you do they will forgive you
And they're always there for you too.

They will always care for and love you
And go on trips with you too.
Some nice people will come and go
But a good friend will always be there.

Mairead McCarry (12)
Sacred Heart Grammar School

MY PET

Quietly in the day
because it is light.
Starts his acrobatics
when it is night.

Playful, energetic
He plays and rides.
Climbs up his tube
and goes for a slide.

Gnawing and chewing
his crunchy treat.
Wants some for tomorrow
so he stuffs his cheeks.

Licking his paws
to wash his face.
Snuggles in cotton wool
his cosy little space.

He has golden, shiny fur
with small dark eyes.
A hamster is a wonderful pet
no matter his size.

Una Montgomery (11)
Sacred Heart Grammar School

THE SEA

The sea came swishing in at dawn
Swish, swish it comes rolling in
.Eating up the sand, slowly, gently
Sliding over the beach.

Swishing, swishing, lapping, lapping
The sea creeps in at dawn
Ever so quiet, ever so gentle
The sun wakes up and says in surprise
'The sea has moved!'

The clouds say 'That can't be'
And they all come rushing over to see
The sea gets grumpy and goes all grey
'Don't stare at me like that if you please
You're ruining my beautiful blue.'

The timid clouds race away
And all is quiet again
'Youth.' grunts the mountain 'Always gadding about.'
The sun smiles happily down at the sea
And the sea shimmers back.

Sara-Louise Cooper (11)
Sacred Heart Grammar School

RUSTIC AUTUMN

The misty skies are forming
All sorts of leaves fall
Cool, chilly evenings are coming
The wind is blowing strong.

The crunch of the leaves are heard
Red, orange and green in colour.
Plants and shrubs begin to die,
The branches start to bare.

The sky becomes overcast
Dusk sets in swiftly.
Long hours of light cease
The sharp cold is in the air.

Animals begin to hibernate
The robin perches on the branch
Small birds commence to fly away
Autumn is finally here.

Carrie-Anne O'Riordan (13)
Sacred Heart Grammar School

I WANT TO BE FREE!

I want to be as free as a bird
Gliding in the light blue sky.
My feathers glistening in the golden sun
Living in a crusty brown nest,
Twisted with smooth brown twigs.
I want to be free!

I want to be as free as a fish,
Swimming through the crystal, clear oceans,
Travelling in silver shoals.
I want to be free!

I want to be as free as a monkey swinging across
the tall treetops.
Hanging from the golden-brown silky tail that I wish to own.
Eating all different kinds of tropical fruits.
I want to be free!

I want to live in peace and harmony, happiness and joy.
I really don't mind about being an animal or a good person
        I just want to be free!

Billie Phipps-Tyndall (11)
Sacred Heart Grammar School

How Does Summer Know When To Come?

How does summer know when to come?
When all the buds and flowers have grown
When all the seeds and bulbs have been sown,
Or, does it just come on its own.

How does summer know when to come?
When the patter of rain has gone away
Summer dawns its first bright new day
Yes, I guess summer knows its way.

How does summer know when to come?
When people want a long holiday
'I'll make them happy,' he'll say
Yes, summer does know his way.

He spreads his rays upon all of us
And unlike winter doesn't make a fuss
And in his way of showing this
He gives us three months of endless bliss!

Emma Kelly (11)
Sacred Heart Grammar School

Dreaming

Where am I?
I'm in some magical land.
The grass is so green.
There're trees everywhere to be seen.

Shhh, I can hear something,
I can hear a soft splash,
It's a pattering sound.
I know, it's the rain pattering off the ground.

There's a lovely waterfall,
It's like silk running down.
The wind gently howls
And there's no hoot from the owls.

There's a lake over there,
It's still and calm.
This is like a dream come true!
What do you think? 'Cause I do!

Donna Mc Cartan (12)
Sacred Heart Grammar School

MILLENNIUM

The clock strikes,
The people roar,
Screaming, shouting,
Smiling, sighing.
Euphonious cheers erupt.
The world embraces.

The clock chimes,
The noon descends,
The stars disappear.
The sky falls
Emptiness envelopes Earth.

Expectant faces await.
Freedom, peace, happiness,
Eternal love.
Expectant faces await.
Imprisonment, fear, war,
Infinite hatred.
Expectant faces await . . .

Joanne Mulholland (14)
Sacred Heart Grammar School

A New Beginning

I've started a new beginning,
In a brand new school,
With lots of different classrooms
And different teachers too.

Irish and French are different subjects,
That I haven't done before.
Along with messing about,
Which I can't do anymore.

I'm always rushing about,
Running up and down the stairs,
Unlike my other primary schools,
St Ronan's and St Clare's.

Now that I'm getting used to it
It isn't really that bad.
But when I think of my primary school,
I can't help but feel sad.

Aisling Gallagher (11)
Sacred Heart Grammar School

Seasons

Spring is when new animals are born,
Spring is when the lark comes out early in the morn
Spring is when the buds come out on the trees,
Spring is when we have friends round for special teas.

Summer is when we are off school,
Summer is when we obey hardly any rules,
Summer is when the trees are bright,
Summer is a wonderful sight.

Autumn is when the leaves are crisp and red,
Autumn is when we go earlier to bed,
Autumn is when the nights draw in,
Autumn is when we sit around Hallowe'en bonfires and sing.

But best of all is when winter comes,
When we all sit cosily in our homes.
And we wait patiently 'til nigh,
For the new millennium to light up the sky.

Elizabeth Kimmins (11)
Sacred Heart Grammar School

CREATION

The sea, the sky and the land,
God made each one by hand.
He made the animals one and all,
He also invented the waterfall.
He made the rain and the snow
And how he thought of sleet, I do not know.
He never forgot the insects, no matter how small,
And they came to him when he sent his call.
He made the man and woman special in every way,
And he watched them grow throughout the day.
Now back to the animals, the birds and the fish,
For them to live peacefully, was his only wish.
The birds could fly and the fish could swim,
And he filled each ocean right up to the brim.
God made everything in a different way,
And he'll make some more another day.

Emma Rose McAteer (11)
Sacred Heart Grammar School

My Hallowe'en Fright

At the edge of dark
on a cold, damp night.
I glanced at the stars
which shone so bright.

The wind grew strong
and guess my surprise
perched upon a broom
with evil green eyes.

A smoky black cloak
a hat like a cone
her cackling voice
I was frightened, alone.

I turned and ran like a hare
until I could no longer be seen.
How silly of me to stroll in the park
when witches are out on Hallowe'en!

Niamh McAvoy (11)
Sacred Heart Grammar School

In Autumn

Red, yellow, green and brown
All the leaves come swirling down.
Dancing on the wind, floating free,
A dazzling sight for all to see.

This is the season Jack Frost awakes,
With his pointed fingers he will make
The world a glittering white.
His eyes are cold, his heart of stone.

Hallowe'en's a time of spooky faces,
Flaming bonfires towering high,
Rockets lighting up the sky.
Children shouting 'Trick or treat.'

Coming into winter season,
Days are cold, nights are freezing.
It will be not too long
Till we hear bird's song.

Aine Crozier (11)
Sacred Heart Grammar School

IN MY DREAMS

When I fall asleep at night
A whole new world stands before my eyes
The birds soar high and sing all day
Where the horses stay grazing in the hay.
There's a lovely smell of the newly cut grass
The sheep bleat happily in the fields as I pass.
Run through the meadows and swim in the lake
Is this real life, or just a mistake?
The flowers stand so proud and pretty
There's a lovely breeze in my face,
How I love this beautiful place.
The blackberries hang ripe on the edge of the bush
While the family of roses are in growth.
Flowing calm and gently is a little stream
I soon wake up and find this is all a dream.

Victoria Kerr (12)
Sacred Heart Grammar School

HALLOWE'EN

The sun is falling,
The night is calling,
As Old Hallow's Eve,
Draws near.
Bats flutter,
Children mutter,
As the full moon starts to appear.
Bonfires flicker in the distance,
Colours light the sky,
Children saying,
'Trick or Treat'
When the candy catches their eyes.
But in silence,
Blocked and hid,
The mysteries of Hallowe'en lie,
For when the clock strikes twelve o'clock,
The witches and vampires fly!

Adele Cunningham (11)
Sacred Heart Grammar School

LITTLE BROTHERS

Little brothers are little monsters,
Bothering you every day.
Always nagging at your side,
Annoying you in every way.

But do we ever take time to look,
And see how special they are.
We never seem to notice,
That they actually do care.

We often think they love themselves,
And are really dirty and rude.
They certainly aren't ever king,
And never have time for you.

So if you have a little brother,
And you think you hate his guts.
Take some time to think about this,
He really does love you much.

Michelle Grant (12)
Sacred Heart Grammar School

THE LESSON

I was sitting in the classroom
One cold and wintry day
The teacher was talking
But my thoughts were astray

I was wishing I was
Somewhere far away
Like on a golden beach
With the sun shining bright
Or in a big busy city
Illuminated by night.

Suddenly my thoughts were interrupted
The bell has just rung
The teacher has finished talking
The packing of bags has begun
It's the end of the day and the end of a week
Now it's the weekend, I can have fun.

Niamh Haughey (14)
Sacred Heart Grammar School

WHEN . . .

I looked up to the heavens,
And I prayed to God above.
I prayed for him, to send upon us
A pure and peaceful dove.

I looked down at the Earth
Why, my blood began to boil.
Was this the place they'd hoped to build
When my fellow man did toil?

When I looked upon our streets
And the tears do fill my eyes.
They hadn't hoped to build a place
Where we ignore each other's cries.

When this had been the land of hope
For every man; each one.
When this had been the land of peace
Without denial, without a gun.

Ruth Muckian (13)
Sacred Heart Grammar School

HALLOWE'EN

Hallowe'en, October 31st every year
So let's hope you've some Hallowe'en cheer
Witches, vampires all out for the night
Over the sweets, little children fight.

Knocking on doors, hoping for sweets
A nasty surprise for those with no treats.
Bonfires, bangers, skies filled with lights
The whole world goes mad for this one night.

Evilness lurks here and there
Children giving adults a nasty scare
Scary masks, costumes, make-up and all
You would think they were going to a monster ball.

Madness breaks out just for one night
Parents are glad when it's all out of sight
They don't like the costumes so they say
But we'll remind them they did in their day.

Ann Marie Moley (14)
Sacred Heart Grammar School

MY DREAMLAND (FREEDOM)

When day will dawn and sun arise,
I'll awake and open my eyes,
I'll pack my bags and off I'll go,
To the land where my dreams will flow.

I'll wander far at peace and ease,
And stop for the night where'er I please,
I'll walk for miles and climb the hills,
And lie down to rest among the daffodils.

The sweet scented smell of the rambling rose,
The perfume from the wild flowers that grow,
The tranquil stream that flows along,
The birds singing sweetly their little song.

This is the place I wish to go,
To let my freedom gently flow,
I hope to reach this place one day,
Where my heavenly dreams are there to stay.

Bronagh Doyle (12)
Sacred Heart Grammar School

THE FOREST

As I entered the forest I could hear
The birds singing and squawking
The owls hooting
And the far-off screaming of some strange
and eerie creature.

As I stepped further into the darkness
All around, leaves rustling and crackling,
Twigs wrapping and snapping at my feet,
And ahead the splashing and lapping of water
flowing through distant rocks.

As I walked deeper into the forest
The foul scent of death filled me with apprehension
The pungent smell of putrefied leaves and decayed corpses
Assaulted my senses from every side.

Out of the darkness a tranquil sea radiated peace and harmony.
Rays of ease fell upon me
I smelt the fragrance of bluebells basking under the silvery
luminescence of the full moon.
With joy and wonderment I had reached the place of my desire.

Cassandra O'Hare (11)
Sacred Heart Grammar School

FASHION PASSION

London fashion week is coming around soon,
All those weird clothes that come from the moon,
Skirts, trousers one of a kind,
The sort of things for different minds.

Yellow, orange, red and blue,
Any style will definitely suit you.
Shirts, tops and bell-bottoms too,
Just as long as they are designed for you.

Watch out it's the fashion cops,
Coming to take you away,
'That skirt does not go with that top!' they'll say,
'Oh my goodness what shame you display!'

It doesn't matter what you wear,
Anything will do,
The most important thing to remember is,
To wear a smile and be true to you.

Claire Hughes (11)
Sacred Heart Grammar School

WEATHER

Sun is bright
Sun is cheerful
Sun is happy
Sun is hot

Rain is boring
Rain is dull
Rain is miserable
Rain is wet

Wind is strong
Wind is cold
Wind is fresh
Wind is soft

Snow is cold
Snow is white
Snow is fun
Snow is bright.

Alison Travers (11)
Sacred Heart Grammar School

THE RED SQUIRREL

Running through the noisy park
With the wind whistling through my hair,
I saw a red squirrel darting up a tree
with a nut in his mouth.

Oh little squirrel, little squirrel!
You are so beautiful
With your long, fluffy tail
And sharp claws.

You are so rare.
Why are your numbers falling?
Store the nuts in your drey
And keep safe, please!

Roisin Donnelly (12)
Sacred Heart Grammar School

HALLOWE'EN

Hallowe'en
comes once a year.
People dress up and try to scare.
Toffee apples and trick or treat.
Gangs of people roam the street.

Witches, vampires, bats and ghosts,
Which of them scare you the most!
Bonfires burning everywhere.
People have lots of treats to share.

A word of advice to people everywhere,
On the 31st of October . . . Beware!

Jenny Morgan (11)
Sacred Heart Grammar School

SUMMER IS GREAT

Summer is here,
Let's give a cheer!
Children shout
And play about,
Oh! Summer is great!

Let's go to the beach
And have a splash!
The sun has come out
And I have no doubt
This summer will be great!

We'll have lots of fun,
Until the day is done
And stay up late every night
Oh! Summer is the best!

The summer is now over
And off to school we march!
Collecting leaves on our way,
Oh! Autumn is great!

Niamh McGuinness (11)
Sacred Heart Grammar School

FRIENDSHIP

Friendship is a good thing,
Let's all rejoice and let's all sing.

We all have friends for many things,
One they share,
Two they care,
And without friends we'd all feel bare.

Dainah King (11)
Sacred Heart Grammar School

HOLIDAYS!

Think of summer holidays
Think of all the fun
Think of all the lounging around
In the midday sun.

Oh to be on holiday right now
Oh how much fun it would be
Lying on a lilo
On the wavy salty sea.

To sit and drink cocktails all day
Would be a dream of mine
Not being in school at all
Would suit me just fine

And although it is only October
I'll be going in June
I'll start my preparation
For those days very soon.

Ciara McKevitt (11)
Sacred Heart Grammar School

AUTUMN

I look through my windowpane
But all I can see is rain,
The wind howls and growls,
The trees shiver
And the water trickles into the river.
I see the rustling leaves fall,
I wouldn't like to go outside at all
And I hear a pitter patter on my windowpane.

Rosaleen McConville (12)
Sacred Heart Grammar School

RAIN

Rain is here yet again
Drumming on my windowpane.
Splish, splosh, he made a puddle.
Making the path look quite a muddle.
Pitter, patter, echoes all around me.
How warm I feel deep down inside thee,
Wind whooshes up and down.
Makes quivering trees swirl round and round.
Wind dies down, soon departs us,
But rain he's stronger.
It can't go on for much longer.
Yet as I predicted he soon follows wind,
He came and went with so much power,
I expect he'll be back with another shower.

Brid O'Hagan (11)
Sacred Heart Grammar School

MY FRIEND

This person is the best
She's better than all the rest

She will help me when I am down
She'll make me smile and take away my frown.

I know my friend is always there
And I know that she will always care.

She means the world to me
And I could have no other
And if you want to know this person
Her name is simply *Mother.*

Charlene Malone (11)
Sacred Heart Grammar School

FOUR SEASONS

Four seasons beginning with spring,
Buds and shoots is what it brings.
Young lambs, calves and birds are born,
Long before spring is gone.

Summer comes with its delight,
Flowers blooming in the light.
This is how the summer goes,
Holidays, outings we do go.

Leaves are falling red, yellow and brown,
We watch them swirling to the ground.
Autumn nights, full of frights,
As we trick or treat on Hallowe'en nights.

Snowballs, snowmen our hands are cold,
This winter season is very bold.
But Christmas comes with love and cheer,
To finish off another year.

Keri Fitzpatrick (11)
Sacred Heart Grammar School

HALLOWE'EN

Horrible monsters and ghastly ghosts roam the streets.
Witches high in the sky searching for juicy treats.
Goblins and ghouls haunting a house.
Ghosts creeping about as quiet as a mouse.

Pumpkins and lanterns lighting the room.
Bats flying towards the moon.
Devils dancing around a fire.
Wizards casting spells with all the things they desire.

Denise O'Hagan (13)
Sacred Heart Grammar School

THE LIGHT

The light so high in the pitch black night
The sparkle is so very smooth and bright

A big, round moon sits up in the sky
If you look closely, a witch might fly by

There's a man on the moon or so they say
But you cannot see him during the day

His mouth, ears, nose and eyes
Are all so perfect in the dark, black skies

Are you shiny, Are you dim,
Are you filled full of gold right up to the brim?

Can you see during the night,
When everyone's in bed and out of sight?

You're in the sky every night during the week
Do you get bored or play hide and go seek?

Aìne Quinn (13)
Sacred Heart Grammar School

CANDLES

C andles range in colour, but,
A mber is the flame.
N ight-time's when we use them
D arkness and in vain.
L ights, they cast a shadow
E ver glowing in the rain.
S ilhouettes they cast upon
    the raindropped windowpane.

Maeve McKeown (11)
Sacred Heart Grammar School

The Wonderful World

The world is a wonderful place
So many people to meet, places to see
and languages to learn.

Some of us stay in our own cosy home
afraid to venture into the real world.
But in reality the world is great
seeing how different people live.
Tasting their food and taking part
in their customs.

Every journey is special
Each country different
And each person unique
The world is a wonderful place.

Gillian Casey (12)
Sacred Heart Grammar School

Autumn

The leaves of the trees fall slowly down upon the worn grasses.
Raindrops trickle down my face as gently as can be.

The clouds are very dull and grey as the day goes by.
Winter's coming, the howling wind, hear it passing by.

The sun is shining brightly upon the beaming flowers.
But thunder takes over with a boom from the stars.

The autumn is nearly over now, all the last leaves fall upon
the meadows and fields.
And now it's time to say goodbye,
I'll see you next year.

Donna Magee (11)
Sacred Heart Grammar School

RUNNING

We ran
We ran through it all
No obstacles
Wide, long spaces
Created for our feet
Yours and mine

I still feel the soft soil underneath me
Digging gently against my stepping feet
My hands gripping yours
Not letting go
I still hold your hands
We are still running
And I know we won't stop.

Niamh Corcoran (14)
Sacred Heart Grammar School

THE SUN

The sun is not out today,
So no one has come out to play.
It is very boring in the house,
Where it is as quiet,
As quiet as a mouse.

It's still raining and the sun is
Behind a big, black cloud.
It's raining, it's raining,
It's raining very loud.

At last, at last the sun is back,
We can now go and pick
Blackberries in a big sack.

Michelle Mathers (12)
Sacred Heart Grammar School

THE RAILWAY STATION

Screeching of the brakes
banging of the carriage doors
clattering of feet
the buzzing of the loud speaker.

I hear all these noises
in my ear as I wait
for the train.

The hustle and bustle
of people running by.

A hoot of the horn
and the rickety rack
and the train screeches
down the track.

Siofra Crozier (12)
Sacred Heart Grammar School

THE CAT

The cat is like no animal,
Which I have ever seen.
Its emerald-green eyes stare at you,
And may seem very mean.
Its fur is like pure, smooth silk,
Flowing through your hand.
Why can't I have hair like that?
I do not understand!
But underneath the cute exterior,
Lies something fierce and wild.
An animal with killer instinct,
An animal with pride.

Grace Gollogly (12)
Sacred Heart Grammar School

A Perfect Dream

I have a dream, or is it real?
A mighty steed reaches over the rail
His long dark mane and well groomed tail
I can clearly see through the hail.

His amazing strength and perfect gait
Calls to me 'Open the gate'
Tack him up at an amazing rate
Tighten the girth, fix the stirrup before it's too late.

Off we go, across the fields
First a canter, then a gallop
No hill too steep or hedge too high
My heart is beating to the thundering hooves.

Lisa Fitzgerald (12)
Sacred Heart Grammar School

Autumn Leaves

A utumn is a time of colour
U nder trees with bare branches
T rees are bare and leaves are crunchy
U mbrellas at the ready
M onths of crunching and crackling
N o more green leaves on the trees.

L eaves are all different colours in autumn
E ven red, brown, yellow
A nd orange
V ery crunchy when you walk
E very leaf is a unique colour
S o go outside, it's autumn!

Kelly Ann Faloon (11)
Sacred Heart Grammar School

HALLOWE'EN

Hallowe'en is coming
The chill is in the air
Bangers, rockets, you name it
Are going off everywhere.

Boys and girls are collecting tyres
And anything they can
To put onto the bonfire
To make the biggest pile they can.

Hallowe'en is coming
The chill is in the air.
Only go out if you have to
Or you will get a scare!

Niamh O'Hagan (11)
Sacred Heart Grammar School

THE OLD MAN

Across the road and up the lane,
In a big house lives a man,
Whose name isn't known to anyone,
He lives on his own, well so it's thought.

He comes out only on Saturdays,
To get his shopping, well so you may say,
He is short and thin with a big toothless grin.

He's got a short black beard,
All neatly combed,
And his hands shake with each step he takes,
His face is wrinkled and his hair is black,
Off he goes now carrying his sack.

Sarah Garvey (11)
Sacred Heart Grammar School

Nursery Nonsense

Hickory, Dickory, Dock
A mouse got stuck in a sock
He squealed and he squirmed
And he jumped and he jerked
Hickory, Dickory, Dock.

Humpty Dumpty sat on a wall
Humpty Dumpty stayed on the wall
Throughout the night
And throughout the day
Humpty never moved away.

Jack and Jill went down the hill
After fetching water
They skipped and played
And tumbled that day
Spilling all the water.

Laura Murray (13)
Sacred Heart Grammar School

The River

Bright blue is the river,
Gold is the sand,
Runs along forever,
With shrubs on either hand.

Autumn leaves are floating,
Some stuck in the foam,
Boats of mine are boating,
Will they come back
In time for home?

Aideen Collins (11)
Sacred Heart Grammar School

AUTUMN WALK

As I take a walk in autumn,
The leaves are red and yellow.
There are fewer people in the park,
As the nights begin to get dark.

The farmer takes the cattle from the field,
And the animals hibernate in small, brown nest.
Everything in autumn takes a rest.
As the cool autumn wind blows gently on my face.

The fire burns bright, bright red,
As we long for summer to come back.
Our summer clothes are packed away
As we wear our jumpers, black and grey.

Fiona McNally (12)
Sacred Heart Grammar School

MILLENNIUM

As the millennium draws near,
People are filled with excitement and fear,
Some are worried about the Millennium Bug,
Others don't worry but laugh and shrug.

'But what exactly is it?' I say,
It's really just another day,
Just one more day, just one more night,
But we all can't help but join in the hype!

Crying, laughing, screaming and shouting,
Sighing, jumping, huffing and pouting,
3, 2, 1, it's here!
This wonderful new millennium year!

Marian McGuinness (13)
Sacred Heart Grammar School

GIRLS

Why are girls always much more mature than boys?
They are well mannered and elegant in their poise,
Unlike rude and mean boys,
All they do is play with their toys,

But girls dress all in match
And never ever would live up to a patch,
Boys play football, hockey and baseball!
They shorten their names such as Pat,
Girls could never live like that!

Girls read books and knit and draw,
Boys would never wait to paw,
Every boy I know does this!
Every girl I know does this!
Except
Me.

Lauren McEvoy (11)
Sacred Heart Grammar School

HELP!

Help! I can't do my English,
Help! I have nothing to say,
Help! I'm supposed to write a poem,
Help! I hate poems anyway.

Some people just get it easy,
The words just flow from their pen,
I wish someone would help me,
'Cause here I am stuck once again.

Siamsa McDonald (11)
Sacred Heart Grammar School

THE WEREWOLF

Teeth snarling
Eyes glaring
I look behind
He's gaining
Run faster, faster,
Can't I'm rooted,
Thrown to the ground
Turn around
He's towering above . . .
Jaws wide . . .
I can see inside!
I scream . . . no sound
He's about to bite
Suddenly
I wake up,
What a fright!

Laura Bailey (11)
Sacred Heart Grammar School

HALLOWE'EN

On Hallows Eve the dead awake,
They rise up from their graves
And the ground begins to shake.
The witches cackle as they fly,
The bats are shadows in the sky,
The werewolves howl at the moon,
Their sharp fangs will claim a victim soon.
Children are safe with their parents at home,
Unaware of the demons that roam.

Shona McConville (11)
Sacred Heart Grammar School

HALLOWE'EN

Hallowe'en is coming.
The nights are long and dark.
The bonfire starts with a bang and a crackle
And in the far distance,
I hear a witch cackle.

The bonfire with its helter-skelter shape,
Smells crazy, it sounds angry.
The tyres roar as if they are sore.
The twigs snap, sizzle and spit.

Children squeal as fireworks screech through
the dark, damp autumn night.
Little ghosts and ghouls, witches and vampires
Appear to dance around
The bonfire
All night!

Sinéad Hughes (11)
Sacred Heart Grammar School

THE NIGHT

The night comes creeping in so slowly
He is so quiet, doesn't make a sound
The sun goes and in comes the moon.

The night fills my room with darkness and gloom,
He spoils my fun outside, I have to go in.

The night laughs softly and warns everybody
That playtime is over
Time to go to bed.

Kylie O'Hanlon (11)
Sacred Heart Grammar School

LONDON

London, exciting, dignified, magnificent and grand.
Trafalgar Square waits with hustle, bustle, and plenty of birds.
The river Thames twists and winds with an air of grace,
Enclosed with construction, forms and structures.
Covent Garden is established, historic uncertain and old.
The toy museum is filled with baubles, dolls, knick-knacks and trains,
My childhood encased in glass.
I'll enter the tubes and be confronted with tension,
excitement, heat and swarming bodies.
The Houses of Parliament will stand in front of me and give an account
of history, a chronicle.
An archive of many careers in history.
Buckingham Palace with its grand appearance is commanding, lofty
and stately.
All this awaits me.

Kellyann Mohan (12)
Sacred Heart Grammar School

DAD

Where can I start to describe my dad,
What can I say about my dad.
Football, rugby, cricket crazy,
Sits all day being lazy.
With two telephones going all day,
The only time he moves that day.
Only laughter, kind and funny,
He's always happy when counting his money.
I'd never be without him you see,
Cos he's the only dad for me.

Emma Storrie (12)
Sacred Heart Grammar School

Hallowe'en Night

On Hallowe'en night,
You might get a fright,
But you have nothing to worry about.

Witches galore, might knock on your door,
Ghosts move silently along,
Bonfires crackle and light up the sky,
Fireworks screech and go high.

Inside the feast is ready,
Monkey nuts, hazel nuts and apple pies I adore,
People shouting and jumping about.

Trick or treaters rattle the door,
I don't know if I can take much more
This Hallowe'en night.

Therese Goss (11)
Sacred Heart Grammar School

Morning Arrives

Morning is coming, it's creeping over the land,
Waking up creatures, blowing the sand.
The owl knows it's coming, it's back to his nest,
He can have a snooze there, that part is best.

The sun is rising, peeping over the hill,
Soon the markets will open and start to sell.

Oh how beautiful this morning looks!
It is too pretty to be described in books.

Catherine-Anne McDonald (11)
Sacred Heart Grammar School

HALLOWE'EN

Witches and wizards
Goblins and elves
Come creeping round corners
So mind yourselves.

Hocus-pocus
Frogs' legs and toads
Spells by the dozen
Witches speaking in codes.

Bonfires and bangers
Hats and cloaks.
It all makes for great fun
In our Hallowe'en hoax.

Helen McAvoy (12)
Sacred Heart Grammar School

MY WATCH

My watch, I would be lost without,
My watch, not literally of course
The tick-tock momentum propelled by force
Why is it necessary? Ah well that's life of course!

My watch, I would be lost without,
Colours chaos, pattern random and unrelated
So uncorrected somewhat like our fate.

My watch, I would be lost without,
No but seriously what's it all about?
The cogs keep turning to the right,
Representing the cycle of life? It might!

Helen Cunningham (14)
Sacred Heart Grammar School

SPLIT COMMUNITY

Northern Ireland
Is a place split in two.
There's us,
and there's them.
Why?
are we really that different?
So we don't follow the same religion.
Who cares?
It's the same God, isn't it?
Why?
That's the blue, white and red half.
We're green, white and orange.
Flags blowing from lamp posts.
Not really a pretty sight.
Why?
Murders, violence, bombing -
Fires, abuse, threats and cruelty.
So many lives lost,
Without an achievement.
Why?
Tony Blair, Peter Mandelson,
Gerry Adams and the rest
Spend their days trying to join us.
But it's slow
Why?
Why won't people come to reason?
Why won't they co-operate?
Why won't they give in?
It would make sense.

Aoibhin Gormley (14)
Sacred Heart Grammar School

ACCEPTING YOURSELF

He sits in his wheelchair
Stares up into the sky
He makes a wish
As a shooting star goes by.

He wishes for the gift of his legs
And to kick a ball
For the feeling in his legs
Won't come back at all.

Then suddenly the strength shoots through his muscles
As a wide smile appears on his face
As he stands up
To explore the place.

The excitement gathers
As he finally stops to think
It's only a dream
Which is starting to sink.

He opens his eyes
Still sitting in a wheelchair
He has all the other senses
And why should he really care?

So accept yourself
You were made like that
You are special
Though you may think you're small, thin or fat.

Deirdre Hughes (12)
Sacred Heart Grammar School

AUTUMN AND WINTER

Autumn is a beautiful season,
It's about leaves.
The way they change colour to
Brown, green, red, yellow and orange.
The way they crunch
When you stamp on them,
The way they blow in the wind.

It's also about fun,
There's lots of it.
You have it with your friends,
With the leaves,
With the wind and a lot more.

But soon it comes to winter,
The leaves die,
They shrivel up,
It starts to snow.

Nearly everything becomes white,
Like the rooftops,
The trees,
The ground
And even sometimes yourself.

But winter is also about Jesus
When he was born
And on his next birthday,
He is 2000 years old.

Laura Greenan (11)
Sacred Heart Grammar School

HAVING HOMEWORK

I hate having homework I think it's really boring
I'll tell you how I know this, because I usually end up snoring
It's torture having to sit in that quiet room
But I guess, for four more years, this will be my doom.

I would rather listen to the radio all day long
Instead of saying French I would rather sing a song
I'd love to scrap it and throw it all in the bin
But then my mum would yell at me 'That's a mortal sin.'

Homework tries my patience
It makes me very sad
In fact it probably makes me, really very mad.
So listen hard you teachers, I'm speaking from my heart
If you don't cut down on homework
We may end up taking on art.

Laura Lynch (13)
Sacred Heart Grammar School

GOODBYE

As I walk down the church path,
Walking to her grave,
I wipe the tears from my face
And try to be so brave.

I listen to the church bells,
Ringing steadily
And the choir singing sweetly,
Their song so readily.

The people come flocking out,
The mass is just over.
They talk, chat and meet their friends,
I stand alone, sober.

The tears come rolling down my face,
Empty is the graveyard.
I stand alone and think
Goodbyes are so hard.

Karen McKevitt (12)
Sacred Heart Grammar School

DISCO DIVA

The bright flashing lights
And the big brawling fights
It is so exciting to be here
But what if I am caught I fear.
Forget about it let's go for a dance
Oh my God I think I've just seen Lance
I think I did, I had better get out
Come on I am going I shout.
I fight through the crowd
God in here is so loud
Where is the door
Oh my feet are so sore
I feel a breeze on my leg
Let that be the door I beg
I made it, I'm out
Well just about!

Deborah Gore (15)
Sacred Heart Grammar School

NATURE

The grizzly bears play in small waterfalls,
While the rushing water enjoys a journey
To the wild ocean depths.
The long grass flows and the deer gallop
In the beautiful, glossy meadows.

The hares hop to and fro, trying to find
Food for rebuilding their strength.
The lively fish leap in and out of small
Lakes while the mighty, tall giraffe
Bends down to drink the local
Refreshing water.

The proud elephants walk around,
Trying to keep out of harm's way.
The lions mark out their territory,
Waiting to make a kill.

Stephanie Redpath (11)
Sacred Heart Grammar School

HALLOWE'EN NIGHT

The Hallowe'en time is coming near
The witches and monsters will be here,
Mummies and vampires will be out this night
Circling us round and giving us frights.

Coin ducking and apple bobbing is what we'll play
And knocking on doors then running away,
Fireworks and shouting is all we'll hear
While dogs and cats prowl away in fear.

Munching sweets and gobbling bars
Drinking Coke and eating Milky Way Stars,
Red ice-cream and green gooey jelly
Will roll and squish in all our bellies.

We'll stay out till it gets quite cold
By this time we'll be asked and told,
Watch TV, get into bed
And dream all about the fun we had, in our head.

Aisling Finegan (11)
Sacred Heart Grammar School

FIREWORKS

The sky lights up in the dark
of night,
With lots of bangs and
flashes of light.
Rockets and squealers fly
into the air,
The loud noises give you a
scare.
The light flashes before your
eyes,
The sparks fall and the
firework dies.
Open mouths gasping with
fear,
Fireworks are over for
another year.

Shauna McParland (11)
Sacred Heart Grammar School

I Dream

Every night I have a dream
Sometimes I don't know what they mean
I dream I will be famous soon
Or I will join NASA on a trip to the moon
I sometimes dream that aliens will come to us
They would come in harmony and not make a fuss
I sometimes dream of unpleasant things
Like getting covered in wasp stings
Spiders crawling all over me
I'm glad that's not reality
But there is a dream I hope will come true
And it can be helped by all of you
A dream of peace and equality
I hope that's what the future holds for me.

Cristin Ruddy (11)
Sacred Heart Grammar School

Millennium

The millennium is nearly here
Time for drinking lots of beer.
Time for parties and lots of fun
Start the countdown with number one.
When we have reached number ten
We'll know it's a new year so we can start again.
The year 2000 is approaching fast
Another year old, another year past.
Lots of changes for us all,
This is the year when I'll find fame.
One thing's for certain,
Nothing ever stays the same.

Claire Heatley (11)
Sacred Heart Grammar School

PARENTS

They make you clean your bedroom
And study really hard.
And then if you do wrong
They turn round and say you're barred.

They tell you what is right
They tell you what is wrong
If they added music to these words
They could change it to a song.

Sometimes they make you happy
Sometimes they make you mad
But to have such loving parents
I am very glad.

Siobhan Heaney (12)
Sacred Heart Grammar School

THE LIFE OF A TREE

The tree starts off like a little pea,
One hundred years later it is grown for all to see,
When the trees' shoots burst out,
The newborn leaves begin to sprout.

The soil lies in a coiled shape around the tree,
The buds on the tree are like keys,
Opening up millions of little leaves,
While the winds are blowing them,
The winds that are thieves.

I treat the tree the way it treats me,
So I have to be as gentle as I can be.

Laura Cosgrove (12)
Sacred Heart Grammar School

A DREAMLAND

In my dreams there's a land,
Where all your wishes come true,
With puppy dogs and blue skies,
Everyone knows you and likes you,
Whatever you may do,
Nobody will know.

A land where everyone's young,
And you never get old,
You can sit in the clouds all day,
With no care in the world,
If only this place was real,
The world would be more happy.

Charlene McVeigh (12)
Sacred Heart Grammar School

MY PC WORLD

Gateway to the future or highway to hell?
For with my new PC all is not well.
The day it arrived well-packaged and wrapped.
Computer desk bought, assembled, so apt.
Dad emptied the boxes, removed all the wrapping
My sister and I so excited and clapping.
Programmes to enter, software to install
What do I do when I can't do it all?
Megabytes and printers, scanners and ram
It makes me feel stupid but I don't think I am.
But one of these days it will fall into place
When I master this thing I'm sure I'll be ace.

Nikki Larkin (12)
Sacred Heart Grammar School

THE SEA

A splish, a splash I'm under again
Away from the world of women and men.
The beautiful sea has me under her trance
The graceful dolphins begin to dance

The coral is sharp and tickles my toes
A little fish swims right under my nose.
The seaweed is like a gigantic fan
The sea lion stands up like a real gentleman.

All of these things are under the sea
Just go for a swim if you don't believe me.
A splish, a splash I'm up again
Back into the world of women and men.

Clare Jones (12)
Sacred Heart Grammar School

HALLOWE'EN

Witches witches all around
If they're not careful they'll
fall to the ground.
Fireworks being let off each day,
Colourful in the sky a beautiful display.
Cartwheels and rockets light up the sky
Everyone watching with wide open eyes.

Children running around the streets,
Knocking on the doors looking for treats
Dressed up as witches, ghosts and ghouls
Hoping they don't have to go back
to their schools.

Fiona McKenna (12)
Sacred Heart Grammar School

WONDERING WHY?

Why should people have
More rights than others?

Why shouldn't sisters have
The same rights as brothers?

Why should white be
Better than black?

Why should women have
To take the slack?

Why do girls have to
Wear skirts to school?

When boys wear trousers
They think they rule.

I never realised how many
Questions there are to ask.

To answer them is
One very big task.

This is only the beginning
Of my wondering why?

What else will I
Wonder before I die?

Tara Morgan (11)
Sacred Heart Grammar School

TODAY

I woke up today
To see a sky,
Full of hope,
Full of joy,
Bright and clear,
Beaming with opportunity.
But as the morning faded away
Dark clouds arose
And it rained, hailed then snowed.
All the happiness
Fell to the ground.
Then dusk set in
And all was gone.
I was lost in darkness,
All alone.
Then little stars shone bright,
To guide me through
This sheet of black
I went to bed tonight
A night of dark,
A night of waiting,
A night of searching for those stars,
To lead me to my morning sky,
Full of hope,
Full of joy.

Jenny Deane (13)
Sacred Heart Grammar School

LADY OF SPRING

Lady of spring awoke last night
She got up, stretched, and said to winter
'You must rest now dear,
Lay down your weary head,
For it is my turn now, to do what I do best.'

And while I slept she strolled along
Through the forests, gardens and fields
And wakened all the trees and flowers
From their winter sleep

And magically, green buds and leaves
Appeared on every tree
And as spring walked through the gardens and lanes
Flowers sprouted at her feet.

She sowed green grass on all the fields,
Embroidered roses down by the stream
And as lilies appeared on the garden pond
Tulips and daffodils waved in the breeze.

Lady of spring made not a sound
As she wove her magic last night
And when I woke this morning,
My eyes met a wonderful sight!
I threw open the curtains,
The world had turned green!
I knew we had had a visit
From the Lady of spring.

Emer Tumilty (12)
Sacred Heart Grammar School

MILLENNIUM!

The new year is coming,
Like the flow from a pen,
Like birds and bees humming,
It comes once again!

But this year it's different,
It's a special event,
Two thousand long years,
Since the gift was sent.

The light of the world
Is still shining through
God's greatest gift
To me and you!

Ann Jennings (12)
Sacred Heart Grammar School